THE COMPLETE

Guitar

— CHORD —

HANDBOOK

— Every chord you'll ever need! —

hinkler

Published by Hinkler Books Pty Ltd
45–55 Fairchild Street
Heatherton Victoria 3202 Australia
www.hinkler.com.au

hinkler

© Hinkler Books Pty Ltd 2010, 2015

Author: Nick Bryant
Guitar Consultants: Warren O'Neill and Doug de Vries
Hand Model: Warren O'Neill
Cover Design: Sam Grimmer
Prepress: Graphic Print Group
Typesetting: Quadrum
Photography: Ned Meldrum Digital
Design: Mandi Cole
Editor: Louise Coulthard

ISBN: 978 1 4889 3003 4

Printed and bound in China

contents

Introduction

This book is a reference for almost every chord you are likely to encounter in your playing. Each chord shape has been chosen for its simplicity as well as its relevance.

For each key, the **chord dictionary** lists:

- three ways to play the most common chords: major, minor, minor seventh and (dominant) seventh.
- two different fingerings for fairly common chords: major seventh, suspended, sixth, minor sixth, ninth, minor ninth, augmented, diminished and diminished fifth.
- one shape for the least common chords: major ninth, 6/9, 7aug5, 7dim5, 7aug9, 7dim9, eleventh and thirteenth.

The **moveable chords** section also includes further ways to play most of these chords as barre and moveable chords. A moveable chord is a pattern that can be played anywhere up the guitar neck. There are either:

1. no open strings in that chord; or
2. open strings that are muted or dropped from the chord while retaining a similar sound.

As you move it around the neck, the chord-type is the same; it is just played in different keys. There are many moveable chord shapes, including barre chords and power chords.

For example, the fingering of an open D chord covers the top three strings and the open D string. If you move the chord shape up one fret (one semitone), it will produce D$^\sharp$/E$^\flat$, but take care to avoid playing the open D string as it will clash.

The great thing about moveable and barre chords is that they use the same fingering for every key. Here's an easy way to work out how to play one of these chords in any key:

1. Check where the root notes are. The root notes are indicated by an orange circle in each moveable chord diagram. A root note is the first (1) note of a chord. In most cases, it will be the lowest note: for example, the root note of any C chord is C.
2. Using the fret guide on page 11 and page 206, work out which key you would like the chord for and find that key's root note. (Of course the best way to get around on the guitar is to know your fretboard.)
3. Move the chord shape to that key's root note and play!

If you can quickly define where a particular note is on any part of the fretboard, you will know where to play a given moveable chord. Eventually, it will become second nature to play, for example, an A major barre chord or a B power chord.

Open chords feature unfretted or open strings. These are often the easiest chords to play and form the basis of most fingering patterns. You will find the simpler open chords at the beginning of each section. As a general rule, the chords get more complicated towards the end of each section.

Some chord shapes don't have the root note as the lowest note, which can make the chord sound incomplete if played solo. These chords are called **inversions** and are useful when playing with a band, as the bassist will generally focus on the root notes.

If you're playing with a group, you may find that some chords are too full and muddy the sound of the band. Here is where you can experiment by dropping some of the lower notes from the chords and concentrating on the top three or four strings.

There are many **variants** within most of the chord shapes. For example, a simple way to play the open G major is to only finger the third fret of the first string and ignore the low E and A strings entirely. You'll drop the low G and B, but the other four strings will still create a full chord sound. The other difference in this example is that the lowest note of the chord is no longer G: it is D.

This is an example of an inversion. It subtly changes the sound of the chord. Chords with the root at the bottom are said to be in **root position**.

- When you begin a chord on its third note it is called a **first inversion**.
- If the fifth note is the lowest, it is called a **second inversion**.
- **Third inversions** are only for chords with more than three notes.

Using the example of a C major chord, the inversions are:

- root position: C E G
- first inversion: E G C
- second position: G C E

Another example of a **variant**, which is perfect for funk and reggae, is to barre the three highest strings with the first finger. This creates a minor triad in a first inversion (begins on the third note of the scale), which you can chip at or strum rhythmically. As you move this chord between the first and twelfth fret, you'll find every key is represented. This chord is the second chord on page 219.

The Secret to Playing Chord Progressions

Play at a tempo that allows you to change chords in time. This may mean slowing everything down. Although you might not be playing the song at its correct tempo, you will train your fingers to change chords to the beat.

This is very important: much more so than playing a favourite pop song at the correct tempo but with large gaps between the chords while you get your fingers into position. You will find that you can gradually speed it up until you are at the right tempo.

A metronome in invaluable for this type of practice and will help prepare you to play and jam with other musicians. This same technique also works for scales and riffs – just slow it down.

Brief Notes On Musical Theory

Here is some basic information to help beginners understand how chords are constructed. There are many books and websites dedicated to music theory, so study those for more in-depth information.

Sharps and flats may be a little confusing at first because they are shared between the note above and the note below. To help illustrate this, it's actually easier to use a diagram of a piano keyboard than a guitar fretboard. All the notes on a guitar look very similar, whereas on the piano, each note looks different. To keep this example as simple as possible, only the black keys are shown as sharps and flats. With advanced study, you will find that white notes can be sharps and flats in certain keys. For example, the E$^\sharp$ (F) used in the C$^\sharp$ major chords and the C$^\flat$ (B) used in the A$^\flat$ minor chords.

Q. Why can white notes also be called sharps or flats?

A. A scale must climb alphabetically. Sometimes this isn't possible if you use the natural name of the note. For example, the F$^\sharp$ scale on page 157 uses an E$^\sharp$ instead of an F natural, as the scale would otherwise skip straight from D$^\sharp$ to F and miss the E. It is also incorrect to go from the F to the F$^\sharp$. See also the C$^\sharp$ major scale on page 77.

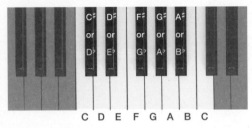

The diagram highlights one octave of a piano keyboard. Count the notes in an octave and you'll see that all Western music is created from just twelve notes, which can be played in higher and lower registers. The white keys have only one name but the black keys have two. Which name is used depends on which key you are playing in. For example, the first black note after C (C$^\sharp$ or D$^\flat$) would be known as C$^\sharp$ in an A major scale but would be D$^\flat$ in G$^\flat$ major.

Each of these black notes has a more commonly used name, especially when talking about pop music. The most common names are C$^\sharp$, E$^\flat$, F$^\sharp$, A$^\flat$ and B$^\flat$. When naming and spelling the chords, these names are used, however each section features both names in the heading and on the tabs at the side of each page. This allows you to find the chord you are looking for, even if you are playing it in a less common key. It should become second nature for you to know that B$^\flat$ is the same as A$^\sharp$, E$^\flat$ is the same as D$^\sharp$, and so on.

Another term used when talking about sharps and flats is the word 'natural'. This term describes a white note when you're also referring to its sharp or flat. For example, if you're talking about 'C$^\sharp$' and then 'C', you can refer to 'C' as 'C natural' to avoid confusion.

Please note that the term 'natural' is also used to describe the relative minor scales. With further study, you will discover other types of minor scales, such as harmonic and melodic.

Minor and Major

The **major** and **minor** scales are usually the first scales learnt in Western music. They are also the scales that all chords are based on. The words 'major' and 'minor' relate to the intervals between certain notes in the scale. It's easier to think of them like this:

- major = large (a larger interval)
- minor = small (a smaller interval)

As a rule, a minor interval is one semitone or half a step smaller than a major interval.

Have another look at the keyboard.

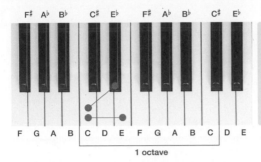

Q. Why are A♭, B♭ and E♭ the only notes that are labelled as flats?

A. Because these are the three notes that are flattened to make a C minor scale.

In other words, this is how these three notes relate to the scale of C major.

- The red shows a major third interval, because E is the third note of the C major scale.
- The blue shows a minor third interval, because E♭ is the third note of the C minor scale and is one semitone down from E: the major third.

Triads

Triad is a term given to chords made up of three notes. Most other chords are a result of stacking extra notes on top of these chords. The basic triads are major and minor chords which you will find near the beginning of each section in the dictionary. Other triads include diminished fifths and augmented chords, which appear towards the end of each section.

A formula can be used to work out how to construct chords in different keys. The formula relates to the intervals used in a chord so it can be applied to any key.

- The formula for a **major** triad is **1 – 3 – 5**, because the chord is made up of the first, third and fifth notes of the major scale. (For example, C–E–G in C major.)
- The formula for a **minor** chord is **1 – ♭3 – 5**. (For example, C–E♭–G in C minor.)

You can see that the only difference between a major and a minor chord is that third note is 'flattened' or moved one semitone down, but both chords share the same fifth note.

Both augmented and diminished chords sound more dissonant (or less harmonious) than other chords because you are drastically changing the skeleton of a chord by moving the fifth note (a much more pronounced change than if you move the third).

- When the fifth note is moved up one semitone, it is **augmented**.
- When it is moved down one semitone, is **diminished**.

Augmented chords are made up of major 3rd intervals (i.e. C – E – G#/A♭ – C), thereby duplicating the same notes (inverted) every 4 frets (major 3rds). Diminished chords are built from minor 3rd intervals (i.e. C – E♭ – G♭/F# – A – C), which reproduce the same notes (inverted) every 3 frets (minor 3rds).

Here are the numbers and names given to each note in the major scale. Bear in mind that these refer to the **position** of the note in the scale and therefore relate to every key.

- **1 or tonic**: first note of the scale; defines the key.
- **2 or supertonic**: second note in the scale.
- **3 or mediant**: third note, which is the middle or mediant note of the tonic triad.

- **4 or subdominant**: fourth note in the scale; named because it is a fifth below the tonic and therefore has a close harmonic relationship with the tonic, as does the dominant.

- **5 or dominant**: fifth note above the tonic; the most pronounced harmonic note after the tonic.

- **6 or submediant**: sixth note and the middle note or mediant of the subdominant major triad; also the first note of the relative minor (see page 9 on relative minors).

- **7 or leading note**: seventh note; **leads** back to the tonic; also the middle note of the dominant major triad, which helps explain why chord progressions often **lead back** to the first chord via the dominant, as it provides a satisfying resolution.

- **7 or subtonic**: also the seventh note but flattened; adding this note to a major chord creates the dominant seventh chord, which is the most common seventh chord in popular music; also the seventh note in the natural minor scale.

The chord dictionary includes a formula for every chord that uses these numbers to describe the note. Memorising the names will be handy for further study.

Here is our keyboard again with the numbers and names that are given to each note, using the C major scale as an example.

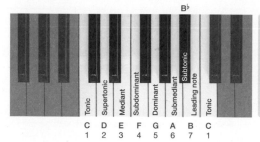

Q. Why is B♭ (the subtonic) the only black note that is labelled?

A. Because adding a B♭ to a C major triad gives us the 7th (or dominant 7th) chord, which is used more often in pop music than the major seventh (which adds B natural instead).

Cycle Of Fourths/Fifths

The cycle of fourths/fifths is great to practise because it cycles through every musical key. The cycle shows some of the patterns that help you understand harmony and the relationship between different keys. This pattern becomes even more obvious if you use the two basic major barre chord shapes or power chords.

Cycle of Fourths

- Begin the cycle at 'C';
- Progress to 'F', which is the fourth chord in 'C';
- Go to 'B♭' which is the fourth of 'F';
- And so on until you come back to 'C', being the fourth of 'G'.

C – F – B♭/A♯ – E♭/D♯ – A♭/G♯ – D♭/C♯ – G♭/F♯ – B – E – A – D – G and back to C again.

Cycle of Fifths

- Begin at 'C'
- Progress to 'G', which is the fifth chord of 'C'
- And so on until you come back to 'C' again.

C – G – D – A – E – B – G♭/F♯ – D♭/C♯ – A♭/G♯ – E♭/D♯ – B♭/A♯ – F and back to C again.

Do you notice the pattern? The cycle of fifths is simply the cycle of fourths in reverse. This helps explain why most chord progressions involve the first, fourth and fifth chords in a key. Those three chords in any key will work together in most styles of music.

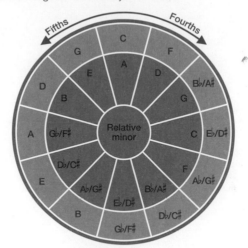

The relative minors appear in the inner red circle. You can also find the relative minors in the outer circle by moving three steps in an anticlockwise direction, for example, from C to A.

Sometimes the 1, 4, 5 formula is shown in Roman numerals so it is written as **I**, **IV**, **V**. Thus we know immediately that we are looking at a formula for the chord progression, which could apply to any key. The roman numerals are shown in the scale grid at the beginning of each section.

The other interesting thing about the 1, 4, 5 chord pattern is that those three chords encompass every note of the major scale of the first (1) chord. For example, the notes of the C major scale are C, D, E, F, G, A, B, C. C is the first, F is the fourth and G is the fifth.

- The notes that make up the C major chord are C, E and G.
- The F major chord notes are F, A and C.
- The G major chord notes are G, B and D.

Every note in the C major scale is represented in these three chords.

This also helps explain why the three-chord theory works. It means that any melody you have in the key of C major can use one of those three chords as the harmonic basis.

Relative Minors

Another important chordal relationship is the relative minor, which is denoted by the submediant or sixth note in the scale. In the key of C major, the relative minor is A minor.

Why is there a minor chord when we are talking about a major scale? Because we can't construct an A major from the C major scale, as the third note of A major is C♯, and C♯ does not exist in the C major scale. Therefore, when playing in the key of C, you are more likely to find an A minor chord rather than an A major.

The basis of the relative minor link is that relative minor scale has the same key signature as its relative major: the key signatures of C major and A minor have no sharps or flats. To play an A (natural) minor scale, use all of the white notes (just like the C major scale) but play them from A to A rather than C to C.

Understanding the Chord Diagrams

This book uses chord diagrams and photographs of the fingering taken from the guitarist's perspective to explain how to play each chord. Explanations of the chord symbols used on the diagrams are listed below, along with tips on how to read the chord diagrams.

 Indicates the regular fingering of a chord and which finger to use.

 Shows possible alternate bass notes when playing finger style (finger picking). You can pick these notes to add more interest. They will usually be the fifth note in the chord but in the lower register.

 Specifies an open string that *can* be played with the chord, but you can decide if you wish to play it or not. These notes are often double-ups that are played on another string, but they can also be very low notes, such the example in diagram 2. They can sound a little strange when strummed with the whole chord. These notes can also add interest when playing finger style.

 Indicates that you can use your thumb to finger the note. This is normally only possible on the low E or A strings. There are a few occurrences in the book to illustrate this technique, which was a favourite of Jimi Hendrix.

 Refers to a string that should not be played.

 Refers to a string that should not be played but can be muted with an adjacent finger.

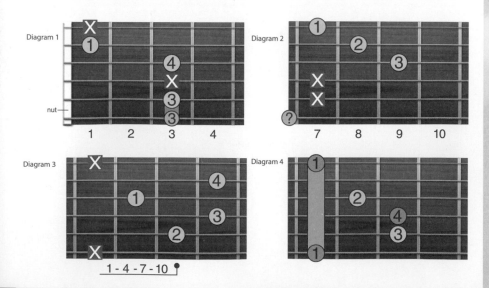

1 2 3 4 The fret numbers along the bottom of the diagram tell you where to place your fingers. Diagram 1 shows a chord within the first four frets, near the nut. Diagram 2 shows the numbers further up the neck.

1 - 4 - 7 - 10 Shows that the chord pattern can be played in several different places up the neck. See diagram 3. You will only find these numbers on diminished and augmented chords, which is due to their harmonic symmetry.

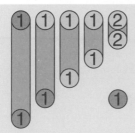

Indicates that you need to finger multiple strings with a single digit. These types of chords are called barre chords. See diagram 4. There are a few examples of barre chords in the chord dictionary but most common barre chords can be found in the moveable chords section. There are no fret numbers in the moveable chords section as these chords can be played anywhere up the neck, depending on which key you want.

Specifies the root note of the chord. This helps you work out where to play the chord pattern in the key you want. You can use the fret guide below, or on page 206, but it is best to learn the notes on every fret for your own reference.

The chord notes are the notes that make up the chord. The chord formula shows the numbers of the notes in reference to their position in the major scale.

The unbolded note refers to an avoid note. This note is part of the chord formula but it is not played, as it causes a dissonance.

Most common name for the chord

Other name(s) for the chord

A11

Alternate Names
A eleventh

Chord Notes A – C# – E – G – B – D
Chord Formula 1 – 3 – 5 – ♭7 – 9 – 11

nut

X

1   2   3   4

Fret Guide

	Fret 1	Fret 2	Fret 3	Fret 4	Fret 5	Fret 6	Fret 7	Fret 8	Fret 9	Fret 10	Fret 11	Fret 12
E	F	F#/G♭	G	G#/A♭	A	A#/B♭	B	C	C#/D♭	D	D#/E♭	E
B	C	C#/D♭	D	D#/E♭	E	F	F#/G♭	G	G#/A♭	A	A#/B♭	B
G	G#/A♭	A	A#/B♭	B	C	C#/D♭	D	D#/E♭	E	F	F#/G♭	G
D	D#/E♭	E	F	F#/G♭	G	G#/A♭	A	A#/B♭	B	C	C#/D♭	D
A	A#/B♭	B	C	C#/D♭	D	D#/E♭	E	F	F#/G♭	G	G#/A♭	A
E	F	F#/G♭	G	G#/A♭	A	A#/B♭	B	C	C#/D♭	D	D#/E♭	E
Fret	1	2	3	4	5	6	7	8	9	10	11	12

A

The A major scale consists of 3 sharps: C#, F# and G#.

The A minor scale consists of no sharps or flats.

The key of A is widely used by many guitarists. A vast number of classic rock songs use this key and it is also a favourite amongst blues players. A minor is the basis of some of the greatest songs of all time and it is also suited to flamenco music.

The relative minor for A major is F# minor.

A Major Scale							
A	B	C#	D	E	F#	G#	A
I	II	III	IV	V	VI	VII	I
1st	2nd	3rd	4th	5th	6th	7th	8th
	9th		11th		13th		

F# Minor Scale (Natural Minor)							
F#	G#	A	B	C#	D	E	F#
I	II	III	IV	V	VI	VII	I
1st	2nd	♭3rd	4th	5th	♭6th	♭7th	8th
	9th		11th		13th		

A

Alternate Names
A major, Amaj, AM

Chord Notes   **A – C♯ – E**
Chord Formula   **1 – 3 – 5**

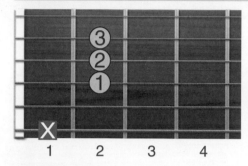

1   2   3   4

A

Alternate Names
A major, Amaj, AM

Chord Notes   **A – C♯ – E**
Chord Formula   **1 – 3 – 5**

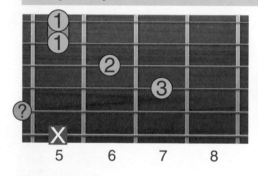

5   6   7   8

A

Alternate Names
A major, Amaj, AM

Chord Notes   **A – C♯ – E**
Chord Formula   **1 – 3 – 5**

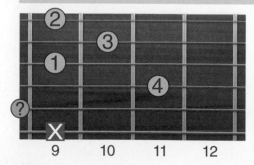

9   10   11   12

A7

Alternate Names
A seventh, Adom7

Chord Notes   **A – C# – E – G**
Chord Formula   **1 – 3 – 5 – ♭7**

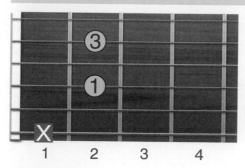

1   2   3   4

A7

Alternate Names
A seventh, Adom7

Chord Notes   **A – C# – E – G**
Chord Formula   **1 – 3 – 5 – ♭7**

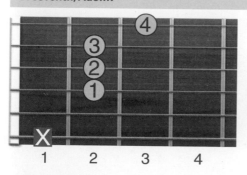

1   2   3   4

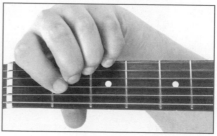

A7

Alternate Names
A seventh, Adom7

Chord Notes   **A – C# – E – G**
Chord Formula   **1 – 3 – 5 – ♭7**

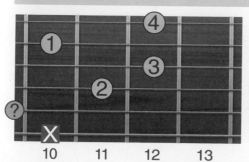

10   11   12   13

Am

Alternate Names	Chord Notes	A – C – E
A minor, Amin, A–	Chord Formula	1 – ♭3 – 5

Am

Alternate Names	Chord Notes	A – C – E
A minor, Amin, A–	Chord Formula	1 – ♭3 – 5

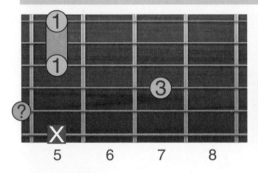

Am

Alternate Names	Chord Notes	A – C – E
A minor, Amin, A–	Chord Formula	1 – ♭3 – 5

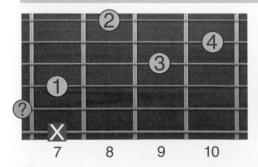

Am7

Alternate Names
Aminor7, Amin7, A–7

Chord Notes **A – C – E – G**
Chord Formula **1 – ♭3 – 5 – ♭7**

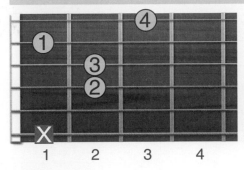

Am7

Alternate Names
Aminor7, Amin7, A–7

Chord Notes **A – C – E – G**
Chord Formula **1 – ♭3 – 5 – ♭7**

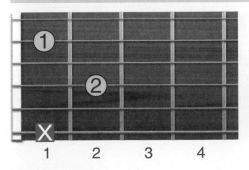

Am7

Alternate Names
Aminor7, Amin7, A–7

Chord Notes **A – C – E – G**
Chord Formula **1 – ♭3 – 5 – ♭7**

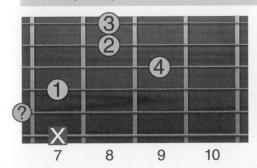

17

Amaj7

Alternate Names
A Major7, AM7, AΔ7

Chord Notes   A – C♯ – E – G♯
Chord Formula   1 – 3 – 5 – 7

1   2   3   4

Amaj7

Alternate Names
A Major7, AM7, AΔ7

Chord Notes   A – C♯ – E – G♯
Chord Formula   1 – 3 – 5 – 7

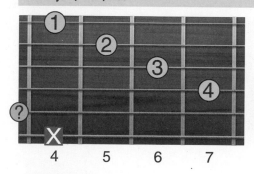

4   5   6   7

Asus2

Alternate Names
A suspended second

Chord Notes   A – B – E
Chord Formula   1 – 2 – 5

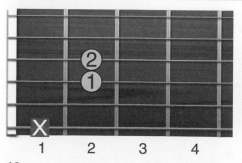

1   2   3   4

Asus2

Alternate Names	Chord Notes	A – B – E
A suspended second	Chord Formula	**1 – 2 – 5**

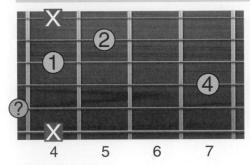
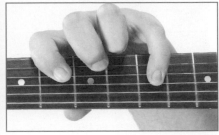

4   5   6   7

Asus4

Alternate Names	Chord Notes	A – D – E
A suspended fourth	Chord Formula	**1 – 4 – 5**

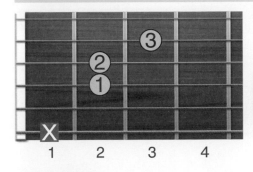

1   2   3   4

Asus4

Alternate Names	Chord Notes	A – D – E
A suspended fourth	Chord Formula	**1 – 4 – 5**

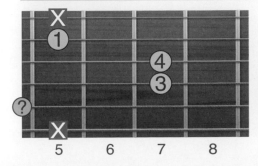

5   6   7   8

A7sus4

Alternate Names	Chord Notes	A – D – E – G
A7 suspended fourth	Chord Formula	**1 – 4 – 5 – ♭7**

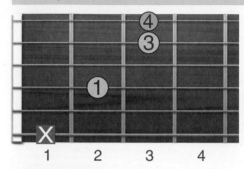 

A7sus4

Alternate Names	Chord Notes	A – D – E – G
A7 suspended fourth	Chord Formula	**1 – 4 – 5 – ♭7**

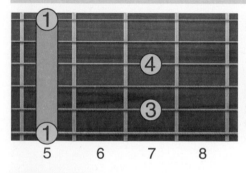 

A6

Alternate Names	Chord Notes	A – C♯ – E – F♯
A sixth, A major 6, Amaj6, AM6	Chord Formula	**1 – 3 – 5 – 6**

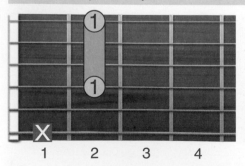 

A

A6

Alternate Names
A sixth, A major 6, Amaj6, AM6

Chord Notes   **A – C♯ – E – F♯**
Chord Formula   **1 – 3 – 5 – 6**

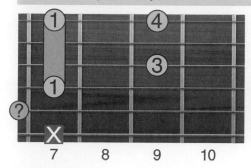

7   8   9   10

Am6

Alternate Names
A minor sixth, Amin6

Chord Notes   **A – C – E – F♯**
Chord Formula   **1 – ♭3 – 5 – 6**

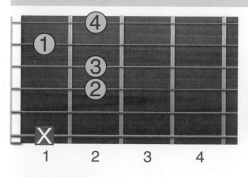

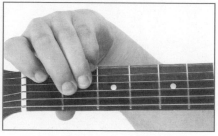

1   2   3   4

Am6

Alternate Names
A minor sixth, Amin6

Chord Notes   **A – C – E – F♯**
Chord Formula   **1 – ♭3 – 5 – 6**

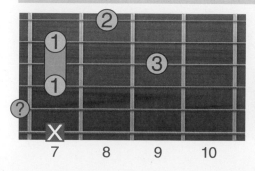

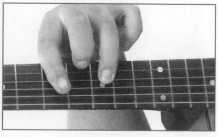

7   8   9   10

A9

Alternate Names
A ninth, Adom9

Chord Notes   **A – C♯ – E – G – B**
Chord Formula   **1 – 3 – 5 – ♭7 – 9**

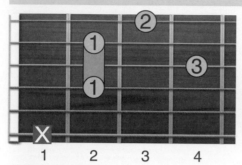

1   2   3   4

A9

Alternate Names
A ninth, Adom9

Chord Notes   **A – C♯ – E – G – B**
Chord Formula   **1 – 3 – 5 – ♭7 – 9**

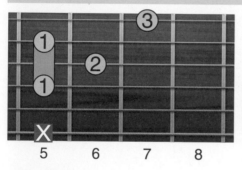

5   6   7   8

Amaj9

Alternate Names
A major ninth, AM9, AΔ9

Chord Notes   **A – C♯ – E – G♯ – B**
Chord Formula   **1 – 3 – 5 – 7 – 9**

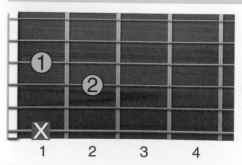

1   2   3   4

Am9

Alternate Names
A minor ninth, Amin9, A–9

Chord Notes   **A – C – E – G – B**
Chord Formula **1 – ♭3 – 5 – ♭7 – 9**

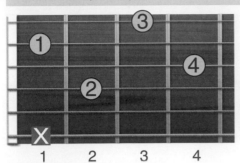

1   2   3   4

Am9

Alternate Names
A minor ninth, Amin9, A–9

Chord Notes   **A – C – E – G – B**
Chord Formula **1 – ♭3 – 5 – ♭7 – 9**

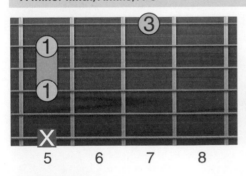

5   6   7   8

A6/9

Alternate Names
A six nine, A major sixth added 9

Chord Notes   **A – C# – E – F# – B**
Chord Formula **1 – 3 – 5 – 6 – 9**

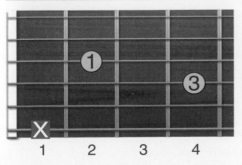

1   2   3   4

Aaug

Alternate Names
A augmented, A+

Chord Notes   A – C♯ – F
Chord Formula   1 – 3 – ♯5

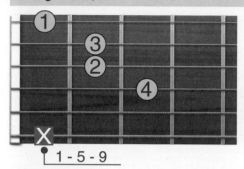

1 - 5 - 9

Aaug

Alternate Names
A augmented, A+

Chord Notes   A – C♯ – F
Chord Formula   1 – 3 – ♯5

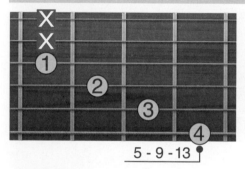

5 - 9 - 13

Adim

Alternate Names
A diminished, A°

Chord Notes   A – C – E♭ – G♭
Chord Formula   1 – ♭3 – ♭5 – ♭♭7

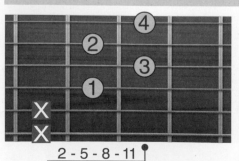

2 - 5 - 8 - 11

Adim

Alternate Names
A diminished, A°

Chord Notes **A – C – E♭ – G♭**
Chord Formula **1 – ♭3 – ♭5 – ♭♭7**

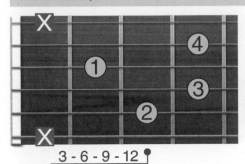

3 - 6 - 9 - 12

Adim5

Alternate Names
A diminished fifth, A–5, A(♭5)

Chord Notes **A – D♭ – E♭**
Chord Formula **1 – 3 – ♭5**

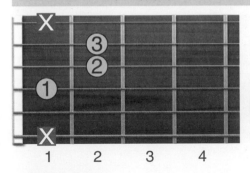
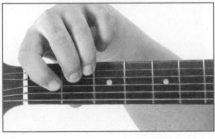

1   2   3   4

Adim5

Alternate Names
A diminished fifth, A–5, A(♭5)

Chord Notes **A – D♭ – E♭**
Chord Formula **1 – 3 – ♭5**

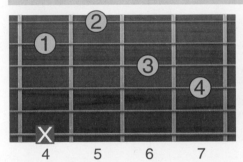
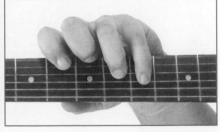

4   5   6   7

A7aug5

Alternate Names
A seventh augmented fifth, A7+5, A7#5

Chord Notes   **A – C# – F – G**
Chord Formula   **1 – 3 – #5 – ♭7**

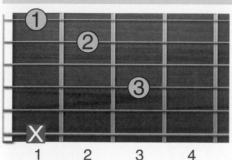

A7dim5

Alternate Names
A seventh diminished fifth, A7–5, A7♭5

Chord Notes   **A – C# – E♭ – G**
Chord Formula   **1 – 3 – ♭5 – ♭7**

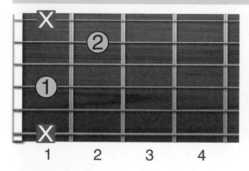

A7aug9

Alternate Names
A seventh augmented ninth, A7+9, A7#9

Chord Notes   **A – C# – E – G – C**
Chord Formula   **1 – 3 – 5 – ♭7 – #9**

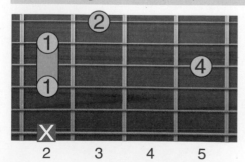

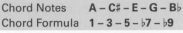

A7dim9

Alternate Names
A seventh diminished ninth, A7–9, A7♭9

Chord Notes   A – C♯ – E – G – B♭
Chord Formula   1 – 3 – 5 – ♭7 – ♭9

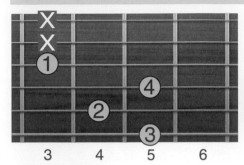

3   4   5   6

A11

Alternate Names
A eleventh

Chord Notes   A – C♯ – E – G – B – D
Chord Formula   1 – 3 – 5 – ♭7 – 9 – 11

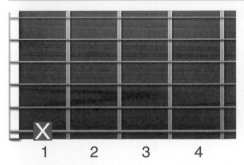
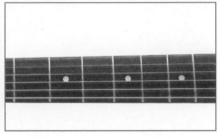

1   2   3   4

A13

Alternate Names
A thirteenth

Chord Notes   A – C♯ – E – G – B – F♯
Chord Formula   1 – 3 – 5 – ♭7 – 9 – 13

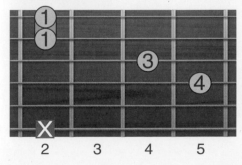

2   3   4   5

Music in the Key of A

Eagle Rock – Daddy Cool

Stairway to Heaven – Led Zeppelin

Tribute – Tenacious D

It's a Long Way to the Top (If You Wanna Rock 'n' Roll) – AC/DC

Get Back – The Beatles

Bagatelle No. 25 in A minor (Für Elise) – Ludwig van Beethoven

A♯ B♭

The B♭ major scale consists of two flats: B♭ and E♭.

The B♭ minor scale consists of five flats: B♭, D♭, E♭, G♭ and A♭.

The A♯ major scale is rarely used in music, as it has so many sharpened notes that it is easier to refer to the B♭ major scale.

The A♯ minor scale consists of seven sharps: C♯, D♯, E♯ (for which you play an F), F♯, G♯, A♯ and B♯ (for which you play a C).

B♭ major is a good key for playing jazz and for accompanying wind instruments, such as saxophones and flutes. Although not an overly common key for guitar, it has been used in many classic pop songs. B♭ minor is known as a 'dark' key, but despite this, many uplifting songs have been written with it.

The relative minor for B♭ major is G minor.

B♭ Major Scale							
B♭	C	D	E♭	F	G	A·	B♭
I	II	III	IV	V	VI	VII	I
1st	2nd	3rd	4th	5th	6th	7th	8th
	9th		11th		13th		

G Minor Scale (Natural Minor)							
G	A	B♭	C	D	E♭	F	G
I	II	III	IV	V	VI	VII	I
1st	2nd	♭3rd	4th	5th	♭6th	♭7th	8th
	9th		11th		13th		

B♭

Alternate Names
B♭ major, B♭maj, B♭M

Chord Notes   **B♭ – D – F**
Chord Formula   **1 – 3 – 5**

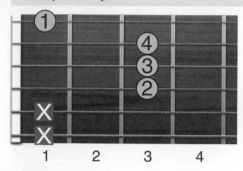

1   2   3   4

B♭

Alternate Names
B♭ major, B♭maj, B♭M

Chord Notes   **B♭ – D – F**
Chord Formula   **1 – 3 – 5**

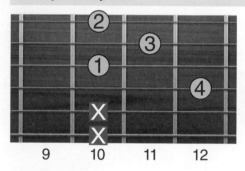

9   10   11   12

B♭

Alternate Names
B♭ major, B♭maj, B♭M

Chord Notes   **B♭ – D – F**
Chord Formula   **1 – 3 – 5**

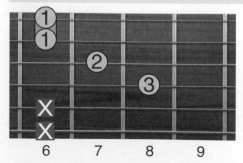

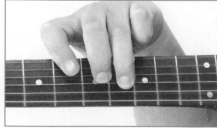

6   7   8   9

B♭7

Alternate Names
B♭ seventh, B♭dom7

Chord Notes   **B♭ – D – F – A♭**
Chord Formula   **1 – 3 – 5 – ♭7**

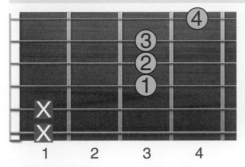

1   2   3   4

B♭7

Alternate Names
B♭ seventh, B♭dom7

Chord Notes   **B♭ – D – F – A♭**
Chord Formula   **1 – 3 – 5 – ♭7**

6   7   8   9

B♭7

Alternate Names
B♭ seventh, B♭dom7

Chord Notes   **B♭ – D – F – A♭**
Chord Formula   **1 – 3 – 5 – ♭7**

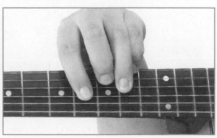

7   8   9   10

B♭m

Alternate Names
B♭ minor, B♭min, B♭–

Chord Notes   **B♭ – D♭ – F**
Chord Formula   **1 – ♭3 – 5**

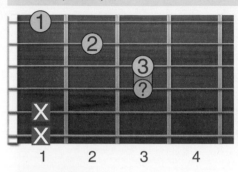

1   2   3   4

B♭m

Alternate Names
B♭ minor, B♭min, B♭–

Chord Notes   **B♭ – D♭ – F**
Chord Formula   **1 – ♭3 – 5**

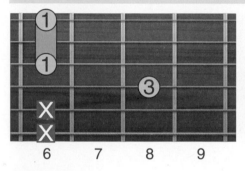

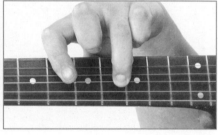

6   7   8   9

B♭m

Alternate Names
B♭ minor, B♭min, B♭–

Chord Notes   **B♭ – D♭ – F**
Chord Formula   **1 – ♭3 – 5**

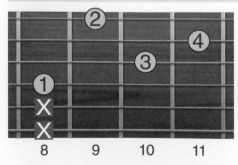

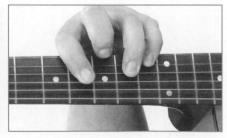

8   9   10   11

B♭m7

Alternate Names
B♭minor7, B♭min7, B♭–7

Chord Notes   **B♭ – D♭ – F – A♭**
Chord Formula   **1 – ♭3 – 5 – ♭7**

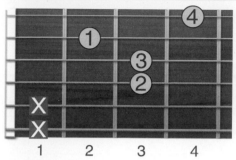
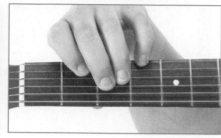

B♭m7

Alternate Names
B♭minor7, B♭min7, B♭–7

Chord Notes   **B♭ – D♭ – F – A♭**
Chord Formula   **1 – ♭3 – 5 – ♭7**

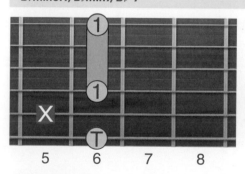
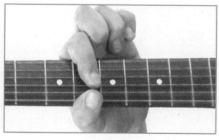

B♭m7

Alternate Names
B♭minor7, B♭min7, B♭–7

Chord Notes   **B♭ – D♭ – F – A♭**
Chord Formula   **1 – ♭3 – 5 – ♭7**

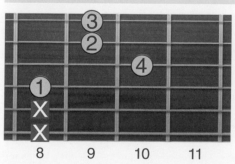

Bbmaj7

Alternate Names
Bb Major7, BbM7, BbΔ7

Chord Notes   **Bb – D – F – A**
Chord Formula **1 – 3 – 5 – 7**

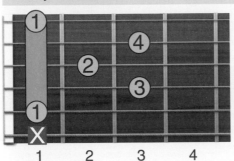

1   2   3   4

Bbmaj7

Alternate Names
Bb Major7, BbM7, BbΔ7

Chord Notes   **Bb – D – F – A**
Chord Formula **1 – 3 – 5 – 7**

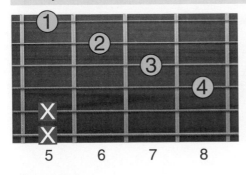

5   6   7   8

Bbsus2

Alternate Names
Bb suspended second

Chord Notes   **Bb – C – F**
Chord Formula **1 – 2 – 5**

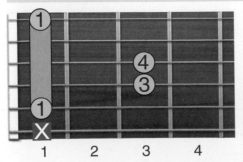

1   2   3   4

B♭sus2

Alternate Names
B♭ suspended second

Chord Notes B♭ – C – F
Chord Formula 1 – 2 – 5

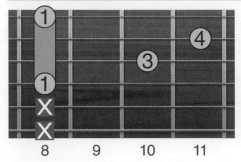

8 9 10 11

B♭sus4

Alternate Names
B♭ suspended fourth

Chord Notes B♭ – E♭ – F
Chord Formula 1 – 4 – 5

3 4 5 6

B♭sus4

Alternate Names
B♭ suspended fourth

Chord Notes B♭ – E♭ – F
Chord Formula 1 – 4 – 5

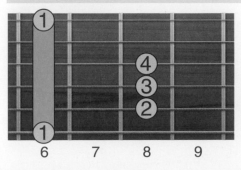

6 7 8 9

35

Bb7sus4

Alternate Names
Bb7 suspended fourth

Chord Notes   **Bb – Eb – Eb – Ab**
Chord Formula   **1 – 4 – 5 – b7**

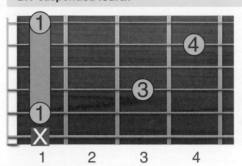 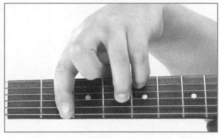

1   2   3   4

Bb7sus4

Alternate Names
Bb7 suspended fourth

Chord Notes   **Bb – Eb – Eb – Ab**
Chord Formula   **1 – 4 – 5 – b7**

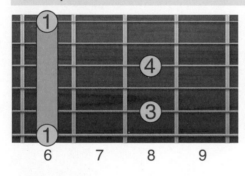 

6   7   8   9

Bb6

Alternate Names
Bb sixth, Bb major 6, Bbmaj6, BbM6

Chord Notes   **Bb – D – F – G**
Chord Formula   **1 – 3 – 5 – 6**

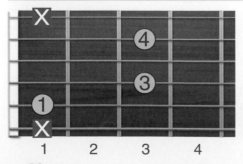 

1   2   3   4

Bb6

Alternate Names
Bb sixth, Bb major 6, Bbmaj6, BbM6

Chord Notes   **Bb – D – F – G**
Chord Formula   **1 – 3 – 5 – 6**

6   7   8   9

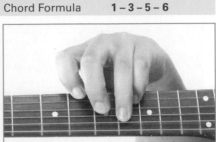

Bbm6

Alternate Names
Bb minor sixth, Bbmin6

Chord Notes   **Bb – Db – F – G**
Chord Formula   **1 – b3 – 5 – 6**

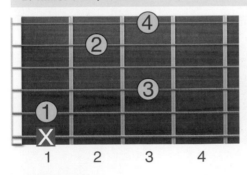

1   2   3   4

Bbm6

Alternate Names
Bb minor sixth, Bbmin6

Chord Notes   **Bb – Db – F – G**
Chord Formula   **1 – b3 – 5 – 6**

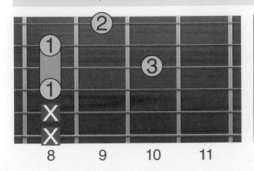

8   9   10   11

Bb9

Alternate Names
Bb ninth, Bbdom9

Chord Notes   **Bb – D – F – Ab – C**
Chord Formula   **1 – 3 – 5 – b7 – 9**

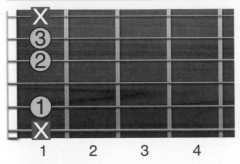

1   2   3   4

Bb9

Alternate Names
Bb ninth, Bbdom9

Chord Notes   **Bb – D – F – Ab – C**
Chord Formula   **1 – 3 – 5 – b7 – 9**

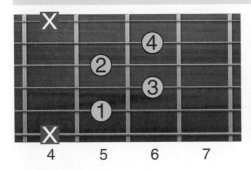

4   5   6   7

Bbmaj9

Alternate Names
Bb major ninth, BbM9, BbΔ9

Chord Notes   **Bb – D – F – A – C**
Chord Formula   **1 – 3 – 5 – 7 – 9**

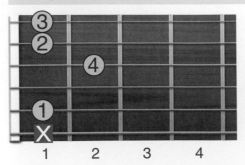

1   2   3   4

Bbm9

Alternate Names
Bb minor ninth, Bbmin9, Bb–9

Chord Notes   Bb – Db – F – Ab – C
Chord Formula   1 – b3 – 5 – b7 – 9

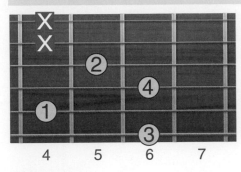

4   5   6   7

Bbm9

Alternate Names
Bb minor ninth, Bbmin9, Bb–9

Chord Notes   Bb – Db – F – Ab – C
Chord Formula   1 – b3 – 5 – b7 – 9

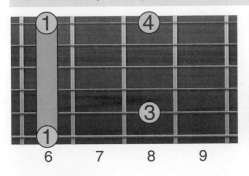
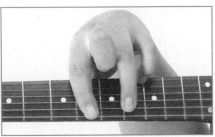

6   7   8   9

Bb6/9

Alternate Names
Bb six nine, Bb major sixth added 9

Chord Notes   Bb – D – F – G – C
Chord Formula   1 – 3 – 5 – 6 – 9

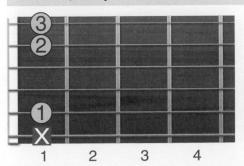

1   2   3   4

Bbaug

Alternate Names
Bb augmented, Bb+

Chord Notes   Bb – D – F#
Chord Formula   1 – 3 – #5

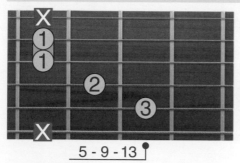

5 - 9 - 13

Bbaug

Alternate Names
Bb augmented, Bb+

Chord Notes   Bb – D – F#
Chord Formula   1 – 3 – #5

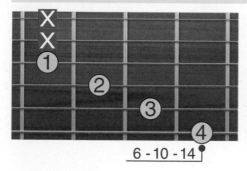
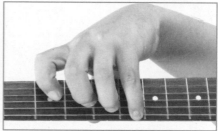

6 - 10 - 14

Bbdim

Alternate Names
Bb diminished, Bb°

Chord Notes   Bb – Db – E – G
Chord Formula   1 – b3 – b5 – bb7

3 - 6 - 9 - 12

40

B♭dim

Alternate Names
B♭ diminished, B♭°

Chord Notes   **B♭ – D♭ – E – G**
Chord Formula   **1 – ♭3 – ♭5 – ♭♭7**

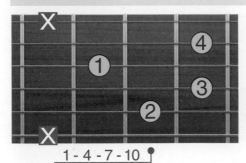

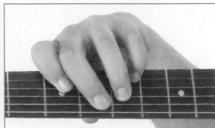

1 - 4 - 7 - 10

B♭dim5

Alternate Names
B♭ diminished fifth, B♭–5, B♭(♭5)

Chord Notes   **B♭ – D – E**
Chord Formula   **1 – 3 – ♭5**

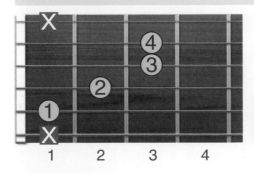

1   2   3   4

B♭dim5

Alternate Names
B♭ diminished fifth, B♭–5, B♭(♭5)

Chord Notes   **B♭ – D – E**
Chord Formula   **1 – 3 – ♭5**

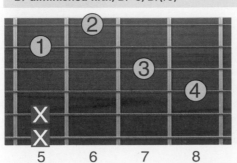

5   6   7   8

B♭7aug5

Alternate Names
B♭ seventh augmented fifth, B♭7+5, B♭7#5

Chord Notes   **B♭ – D – F# – A♭**
Chord Formula   **1 – 3 – #5 – ♭7**

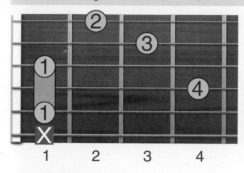
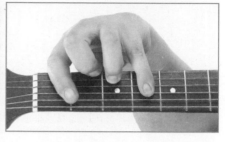

B♭7dim5

Alternate Names
B♭ seventh diminished fifth, B♭7–5, B♭7♭5

Chord Notes   **B♭ – D – E – A♭**
Chord Formula   **1 – 3 – ♭5 – ♭7**

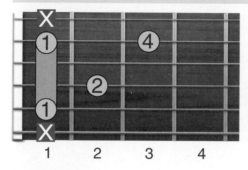

B♭7aug9

Alternate Names
B♭ seventh augmented ninth, B♭7+9, B♭7#9

Chord Notes   **B♭ – D – F – A♭ – C#**
Chord Formula   **1 – 3 – 5 – ♭7 – #9**

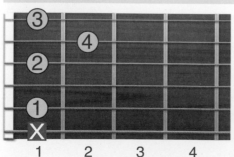

Bb7dim9

Alternate Names
Bb seventh diminished ninth, Bb7–9, Bb7b9

Chord Notes   **Bb – D – F – Ab – B**
Chord Formula   **1 – 3 – 5 – b7 – b9**

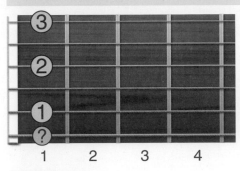

1   2   3   4

Bb11

Alternate Names
Bb eleventh

Chord Notes   **Bb – D – F – Ab – C – Eb**
Chord Formula   **1 – 3 – 5 – b7 – 9 – 11**

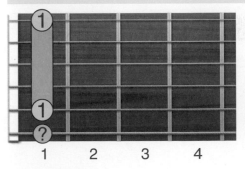

1   2   3   4

Bb13

Alternate Names
Bb thirteenth

Chord Notes   **Bb – D – F – Ab – C – G**
Chord Formula   **1 – 3 – 5 – b7 – 9 – 13**

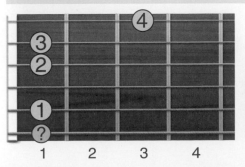

1   2   3   4

43

Music in the Key of A♯/B♭

Revolution – The Beatles

Every Breath You Take – The Police

Breaking the Girl – Red Hot Chili Peppers

Black Hole Sun – Soundgarden

Purple Rain – Prince

Rhapsody In Blue – George Gershwin

Piano Sonata No. 2 in B-flat minor, Op. 35 (Funeral March) – Frédéric Chopin

B

The B major scale consists of five sharps: C♯, D♯, F♯, G♯ and A♯.

The B minor scale consists of two sharps: F♯ and C♯.

B is a key that is well suited to rock, punk and metal. It can invoke passion, rage and fury. The lowest note on a 7-string guitar is tuned to B, which has inspired nu metal pioneers from the late '90s and beyond. B minor has a solemn sound and features a yearning quality.

The relative minor for B major is G♯ minor.

B Major Scale							
B	C♯	D♯	E	F♯	G♯	A♯	B
I	II	III	IV	V	VI	VII	I
1st	2nd	3rd	4th	5th	6th	7th	8th
	9th		11th		13th		

G♯ Minor Scale (Natural Minor)							
G♯	A♯	B	C♯	D♯	E	F♯	G♯
I	II	III	IV	V	VI	VII	I
1st	2nd	♭3rd	4th	5th	♭6th	♭7th	8th
	9th		11th		13th		

B

Alternate Names
B major, Bmaj, BM

Chord Notes   **B – D♯ – F♯**
Chord Formula   **1 – 3 – 5**

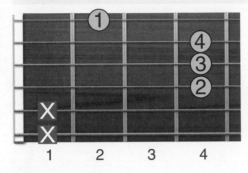

1   2   3   4

B

Alternate Names
B major, Bmaj, BM

Chord Notes   **B – D♯ – F♯**
Chord Formula   **1 – 3 – 5**

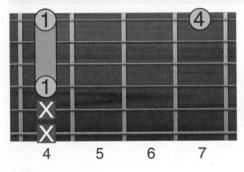

4   5   6   7

B

Alternate Names
B major, Bmaj, BM

Chord Notes   **B – D♯ – F♯**
Chord Formula   **1 – 3 – 5**

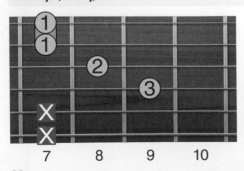

7   8   9   10

46

B7

Alternate Names
B seventh, Bdom7

Chord Notes   **B – D# – F# – A**
Chord Formula   **1 – 3 – 5 – ♭7**

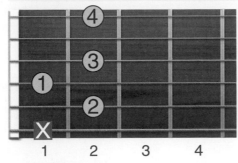

1   2   3   4

B7

Alternate Names
B seventh, Bdom7

Chord Notes   **B – D# – F# – A**
Chord Formula   **1 – 3 – 5 – ♭7**

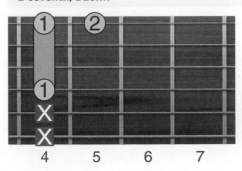

4   5   6   7

B7

Alternate Names
B seventh, Bdom7

Chord Notes   **B – D# – F# – A**
Chord Formula   **1 – 3 – 5 – ♭7**

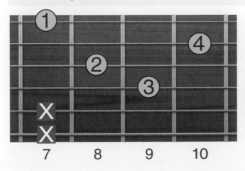

7   8   9   10

Bm

Alternate Names
B minor, Bmin, B–

Chord Notes   **B – D – F#**
Chord Formula   **1 – ♭3 – 5**

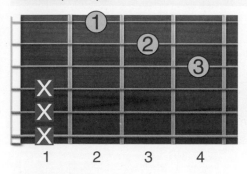

1   2   3   4

Bm

Alternate Names
B minor, Bmin, B–

Chord Notes   **B – D – F#**
Chord Formula   **1 – ♭3 – 5**

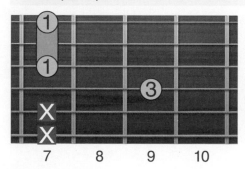

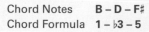

7   8   9   10

Bm

Alternate Names
B minor, Bmin, B–

Chord Notes   **B – D – F#**
Chord Formula   **1 – ♭3 – 5**

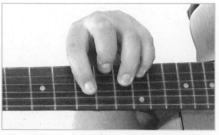

9   10   11   12

Bm7

Alternate Names
Bminor7, Bmin7, B–7

Chord Notes   **B – D – F♯ – A**
Chord Formula   **1 – ♭3 – 5 – ♭7**

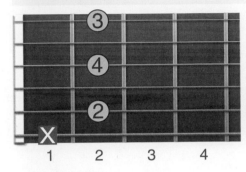

Bm7

Alternate Names
Bminor7, Bmin7, B–7

Chord Notes   **B – D – F♯ – A**
Chord Formula   **1 – ♭3 – 5 – ♭7**

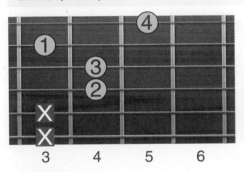

Bm7

Alternate Names
Bminor7, Bmin7, B–7

Chord Notes   **B – D – F♯ – A**
Chord Formula   **1 – ♭3 – 5 – ♭7**

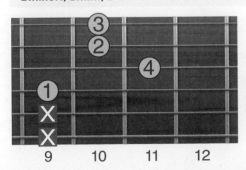
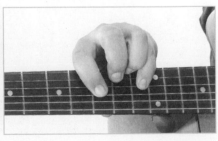

B

Bmaj7

Alternate Names
B Major7, BM7, BΔ7

Chord Notes   **B – D♯ – F♯ – A♯**
Chord Formula **1 – 3 – 5 – 7**

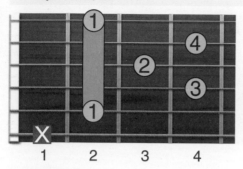

Bmaj7

Alternate Names
B Major7, BM7, BΔ7

Chord Notes   **B – D♯ – F♯ – A♯**
Chord Formula **1 – 3 – 5 – 7**

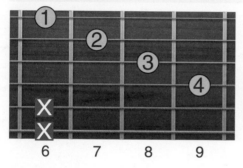
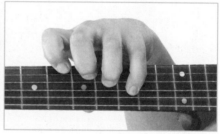

Bsus2

Alternate Names
B suspended second

Chord Notes   **B – C♯ – F♯**
Chord Formula **1 – 2 – 5**

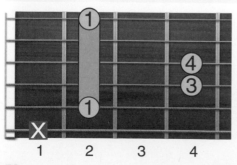
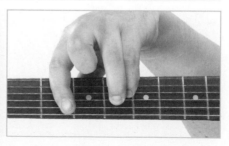

Bsus2

Alternate Names
B suspended second

Chord Notes   **B – C♯ – F♯**
Chord Formula   **1 – 2 – 5**

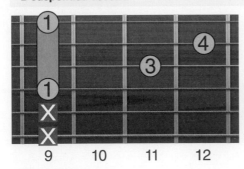

9   10   11   12

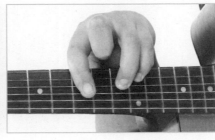

Bsus4

Alternate Names
B suspended fourth

Chord Notes   **B – E – F♯**
Chord Formula   **1 – 4 – 5**

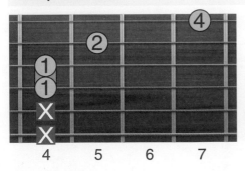

4   5   6   7

Bsus4

Alternate Names
B suspended fourth

Chord Notes   **B – E – F♯**
Chord Formula   **1 – 4 – 5**

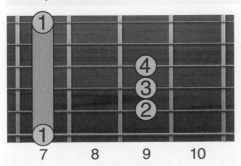

7   8   9   10

B

B7sus4

Alternate Names
B7 suspended fourth

Chord Notes   **B – E – F# – A**
Chord Formula   **1 – 4 – 5 – ♭7**

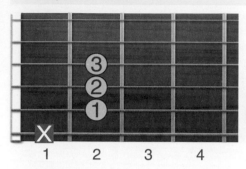 

| 1 | 2 | 3 | 4 |

B7sus4

Alternate Names
B7 suspended fourth

Chord Notes   **B – E – F# – A**
Chord Formula   **1 – 4 – 5 – ♭7**

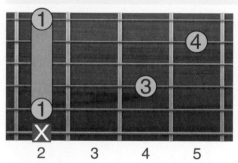 

| 2 | 3 | 4 | 5 |

B6

Alternate Names
B sixth, B major 6, Bmaj6, BM6

Chord Notes   **B – D# – F# – G#**
Chord Formula   **1 – 3 – 5 – 6**

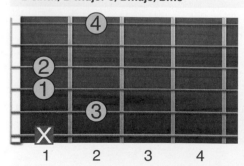 

| 1 | 2 | 3 | 4 |

B6

Alternate Names
B sixth, B major 6, Bmaj6, BM6

Chord Notes **B – D♯ – F♯ – G♯**
Chord Formula **1 – 3 – 5 – 6**

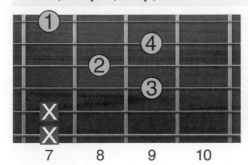

7   8   9   10

Bm6

Alternate Names
B minor sixth, Bmin6

Chord Notes **B – D – F♯ – G♯**
Chord Formula **1 – ♭3 – 5 – 6**

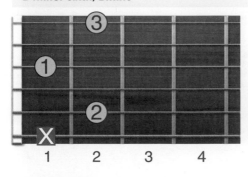

1   2   3   4

Bm6

Alternate Names
B minor sixth, Bmin6

Chord Notes **B – D – F♯ – G♯**
Chord Formula **1 – ♭3 – 5 – 6**

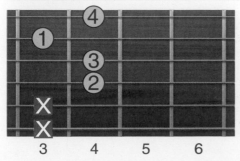

3   4   5   6

B

B9

Alternate Names
B ninth, Bdom9

Chord Notes   **B – D# – F# – A – C#**
Chord Formula   **1 – 3 – 5 – ♭7 – 9**

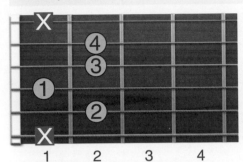

1   2   3   4

B9

Alternate Names
B ninth, Bdom9

Chord Notes   **B – D# – F# – A – C#**
Chord Formula   **1 – 3 – 5 – ♭7 – 9**

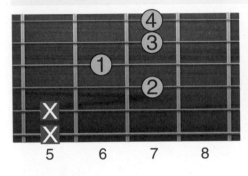

5   6   7   8

Bmaj9

Alternate Names
B major ninth, BM9, BΔ9

Chord Notes   **B – D# – F# – A# – C#**
Chord Formula   **1 – 3 – 5 – 7 – 9**

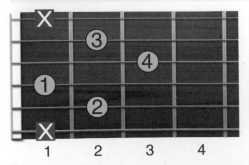

1   2   3   4

Bm9

Alternate Names
B minor ninth, Bmin9, B–9

Chord Notes   **B – D – F# – A – C#**
Chord Formula   **1 – ♭3 – 5 – ♭7 – 9**

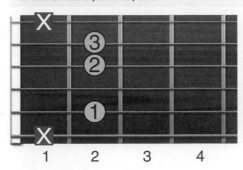

1   2   3   4

Bm9

Alternate Names
B minor ninth, Bmin9, B–9

Chord Notes   **B – D – F# – A – C#**
Chord Formula   **1 – ♭3 – 5 – ♭7 – 9**

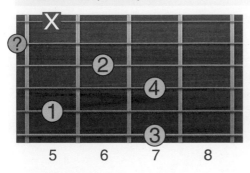

5   6   7   8

B6/9

Alternate Names
B six nine, B major sixth added 9

Chord Notes   **B – D# – F# – G – C#**
Chord Formula   **1 – 3 – 5 – 6 – 9**

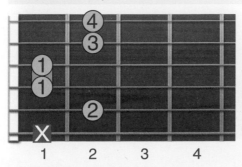

1   2   3   4

Baug

Alternate Names
B augmented, B+

Chord Notes **B – D♯ – G**
Chord Formula **1 – 3 – ♯5**

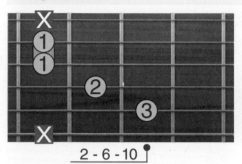
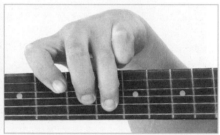

2 - 6 - 10

Baug

Alternate Names
B augmented, B+

Chord Notes **B – D♯ – G**
Chord Formula **1 – 3 – ♯5**

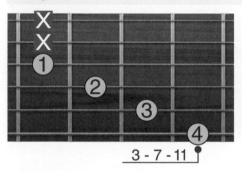

3 - 7 - 11

Bdim

Alternate Names
B diminished, B°

Chord Notes **B – D – F – A♭**
Chord Formula **1 – ♭3 – ♭5 – ♭♭7**

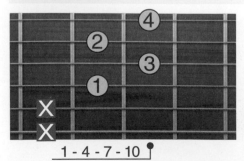

1 - 4 - 7 - 10

Bdim

Alternate Names
B diminished, B°

Chord Notes   **B – D – F – A♭**
Chord Formula   **1 – ♭3 – ♭5 – ♭♭7**

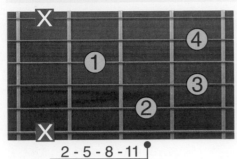

2 - 5 - 8 - 11

Bdim5

Alternate Names
B diminished fifth, B–5, B(♭5)

Chord Notes   **B – D♯ – F**
Chord Formula   **1 – 3 – ♭5**

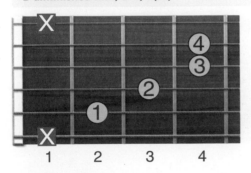

1   2   3   4

Bdim5

Alternate Names
B diminished fifth, B–5, B(♭5)

Chord Notes   **B – D♯ – F**
Chord Formula   **1 – 3 – ♭5**

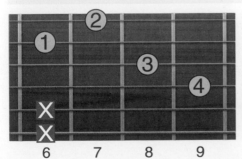

6   7   8   9

B

57

B7aug5

B

Alternate Names
B seventh augmented fifth, B7+5, B7♯5

Chord Notes   **B – D♯ – G – A**
Chord Formula   **1 – 3 – ♯5 – ♭7**

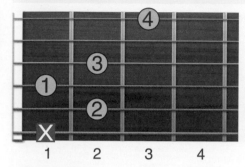

1   2   3   4

B7dim5

Alternate Names
B seventh diminished fifth, B7–5, B7♭5

Chord Notes   **B – D♯ – F – A**
Chord Formula   **1 – 3 – ♭5 – ♭7**

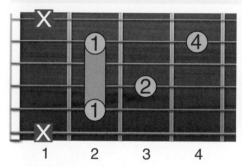

1   2   3   4

B7aug9

Alternate Names
B seventh augmented ninth, B7+9, B7♯9

Chord Notes   **B – D♯ – F♯ – A – D**
Chord Formula   **1 – 3 – 5 – ♭7 – ♯9**

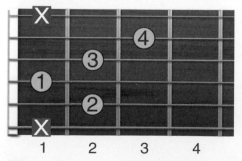

1   2   3   4

B7dim9

Alternate Names
B seventh diminished ninth, B7–9, B7♭9

Chord Notes **B – D♯ – F♯ – A – C**
Chord Formula **1 – 3 – 5 – ♭7 – ♭9**

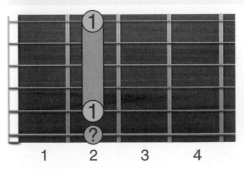

1   2   3   4

B11

Alternate Names
B eleventh

Chord Notes **B – D♯ – F♯ – A – C♯ – E**
Chord Formula **1 – 3 – 5 – ♭7 – 9 – 11**

1   2   3   4

B13

Alternate Names
B thirteenth

Chord Notes **B – D♯ – F♯ – A – C♯ – G♯**
Chord Formula **1 – 3 – 5 – ♭7 – 9 – 13**

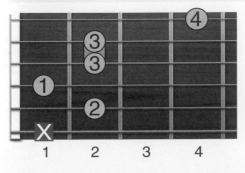

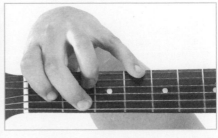

1   2   3   4

Music in the Key of B

Hotel California – The Eagles

One After 909 – The Beatles

Love Rears Its Ugly Head – Living Colour

Always with Me, Always with You – Joe Satriani

Ironic – Alanis Morissette

In The Hall Of The Mountain King, Peer Gynt Suite No. 1 – Edvard Grieg

C

The C major scale consists of no sharps or flats.

The C minor scale consists of three flats: B♭, E♭ and A♭.

The C major scale is popular for country songs, nursery rhymes and lullabies. Many classic pop songs are written in this key. The piano is tuned in C. C minor is also extensively used in jazz, blues and classical pieces.

The relative minor for C major is A minor.

C Major Scale							
C	D	E	F	G	A	B	C
I	II	III	IV	V	VI	VII	I
1st	2nd	3rd	4th	5th	6th	7th	8th
	9th		11th		13th		

A Minor Scale (Natural Minor)							
A	B	C	D	E	F	G	A
I	II	III	IV	V	VI	VII	I
1st	2nd	♭3rd	4th	5th	♭6th	♭7th	8th
	9th		11th		13th		

C

Alternate Names
C major, Cmaj, CM

Chord Notes **C – E – G**
Chord Formula **1 – 3 – 5**

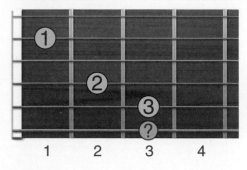

1   2   3   4

C

Alternate Names
C major, Cmaj, CM

Chord Notes **C – E – G**
Chord Formula **1 – 3 – 5**

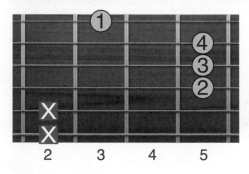

2   3   4   5

C

Alternate Names
C major, Cmaj, CM

Chord Notes **C – E – G**
Chord Formula **1 – 3 – 5**

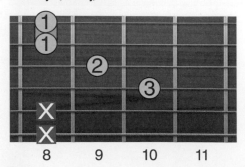

8   9   10   11

C

C7

Alternate Names
C seventh, Cdom7

Chord Notes   **C – E – G – B♭**
Chord Formula   **1 – 3 – 5 – ♭7**

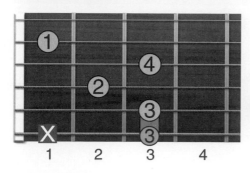

1   2   3   4

C7

Alternate Names
C seventh, Cdom7

Chord Notes   **C – E – G – B♭**
Chord Formula   **1 – 3 – 5 – ♭7**

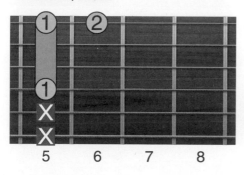

5   6   7   8

C7

Alternate Names
C seventh, Cdom7

Chord Notes   **C – E – G – B♭**
Chord Formula   **1 – 3 – 5 – ♭7**

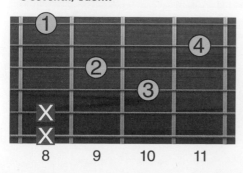

8   9   10   11

C

Cm

Alternate Names
C minor, Cmin, C–

Chord Notes   **C – E♭ – G**
Chord Formula   **1 – ♭3 – 5**

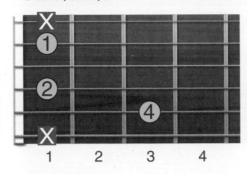

C

1   2   3   4

Cm

Alternate Names
C minor, Cmin, C–

Chord Notes   **C – E♭ – G**
Chord Formula   **1 – ♭3 – 5**

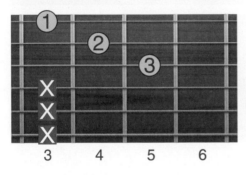

3   4   5   6

Cm

Alternate Names
C minor, Cmin, C–

Chord Notes   **C – E♭ – G**
Chord Formula   **1 – ♭3 – 5**

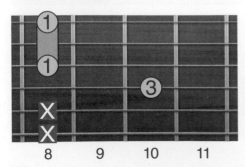

8   9   10   11

Cm7

Alternate Names
Cminor7, Cmin7, C–7

Chord Notes **C – E♭ – G – B♭**
Chord Formula **1 – ♭3 – 5 – ♭7**

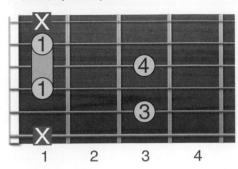

1   2   3   4

Cm7

Alternate Names
Cminor7, Cmin7, C–7

Chord Notes **C – E♭ – G – B♭**
Chord Formula **1 – ♭3 – 5 – ♭7**

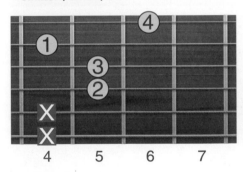

4   5   6   7

Cm7

Alternate Names
Cminor7, Cmin7, C–7

Chord Notes **C – E♭ – G – B♭**
Chord Formula **1 – ♭3 – 5 – ♭7**

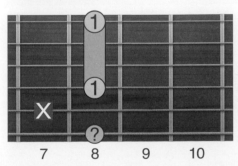

7   8   9   10

C

Cmaj7

Alternate Names
C Major7, CM7, CΔ7

Chord Notes   **C – E – G – B**
Chord Formula   **1 – 3 – 5 – 7**

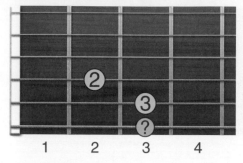

Cmaj7

Alternate Names
C Major7, CM7, CΔ7

Chord Notes   **C – E – G – B**
Chord Formula   **1 – 3 – 5 – 7**

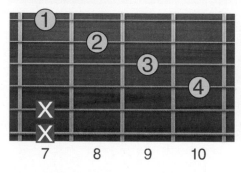

Csus2

Alternate Names
C suspended second

Chord Notes   **C – D – G**
Chord Formula   **1 – 2 – 5**

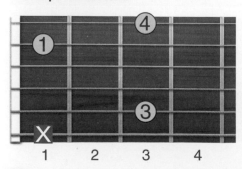

Csus2

Alternate Names
C suspended second

Chord Notes   **C – D – G**
Chord Formula   **1 – 2 – 5**

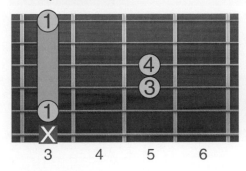

Csus4

Alternate Names
C suspended fourth

Chord Notes   **C – F – G**
Chord Formula   **1 – 4 – 5**

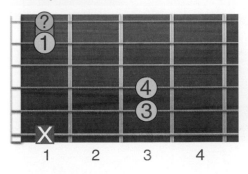

Csus4

Alternate Names
C suspended fourth

Chord Notes   **C – F – G**
Chord Formula   **1 – 4 – 5**

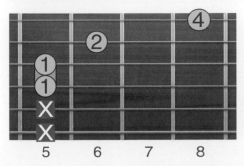

C

C7sus4

Alternate Names
C7 suspended fourth

Chord Notes   **C – F – G – B♭**
Chord Formula   **1 – 4 – 5 – ♭7**

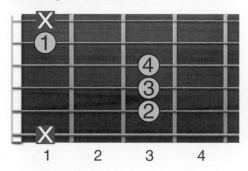

C7sus4

Alternate Names
C7 suspended fourth

Chord Notes   **C – F – G – B♭**
Chord Formula   **1 – 4 – 5 – ♭7**

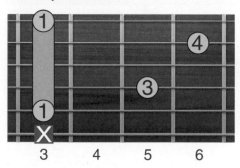

C6

Alternate Names
C sixth, C major 6, Cmaj6, CM6

Chord Notes   **C – E – G – A**
Chord Formula   **1 – 3 – 5 – 6**

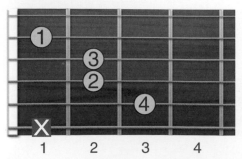

C6

Alternate Names
C sixth, C major 6, Cmaj6, CM6

Chord Notes   **C – E – G – A**
Chord Formula   **1 – 3 – 5 – 6**

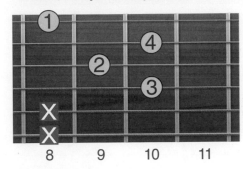

8   9   10   11

C

Cm6

Alternate Names
C minor sixth, Cmin6

Chord Notes   **C – E♭ – G – A**
Chord Formula   **1 – ♭3 – 5 – 6**

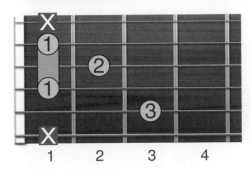

1   2   3   4

Cm6

Alternate Names
C minor sixth, Cmin6

Chord Notes   **C – E♭ – G – A**
Chord Formula   **1 – ♭3 – 5 – 6**

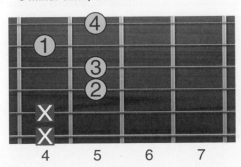

4   5   6   7

C9

Alternate Names
C ninth, Cdom9

Chord Notes   **C – E – G – B♭ – D**
Chord Formula   **1 – 3 – 5 – ♭7 – 9**

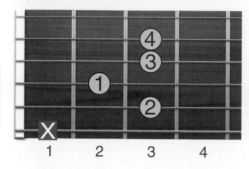

C9

Alternate Names
C ninth, Cdom9

Chord Notes   **C – E – G – B♭ – D**
Chord Formula   **1 – 3 – 5 – ♭7 – 9**

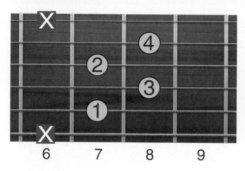

Cmaj9

Alternate Names
C major ninth, CM9, CΔ9

Chord Notes   **C – E – G – B – D**
Chord Formula   **1 – 3 – 5 – 7 – 9**

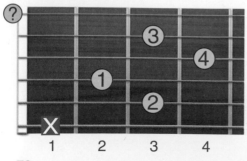

Cm9

Alternate Names
C minor ninth, Cmin9, C–9

Chord Notes   **C – E♭ – G – B♭ – D**
Chord Formula **1 – ♭3 – 5 – ♭7 – 9**

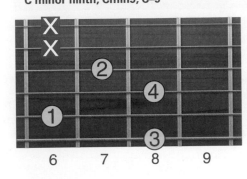

6   7   8   9

Cm9

Alternate Names
C minor ninth, Cmin9, C–9

Chord Notes   **C – E♭ – G – B♭ – D**
Chord Formula **1 – ♭3 – 5 – ♭7 – 9**

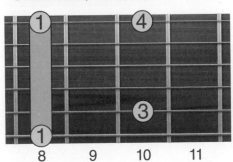

8   9   10   11

C6/9

Alternate Names
C six nine, C major sixth added 9

Chord Notes   **C – E – G – A – D**
Chord Formula **1 – 3 – 5 – 6 – 9**

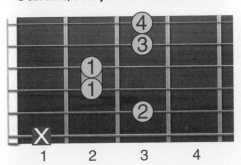

1   2   3   4

C

Caug

Alternate Names
C augmented, C+

Chord Notes   **C – E – G♯**
Chord Formula   **1 – 3 – ♯5**

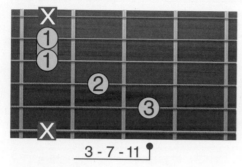

3 - 7 - 11

Caug

Alternate Names
C augmented, C+

Chord Notes   **C – E – G♯**
Chord Formula   **1 – 3 – ♯5**

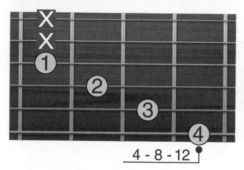

4 - 8 - 12

Cdim

Alternate Names
C diminished, C°

Chord Notes   **C – E♭ – G♭ – A**
Chord Formula   **1 – ♭3 – ♭5 – ♭♭7**

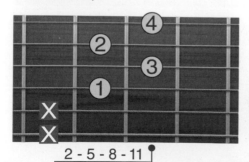

2 - 5 - 8 - 11

C

Cdim

Alternate Names
C diminished, C°

Chord Notes   **C – E♭ – G♭ – A**
Chord Formula **1 – ♭3 – ♭5 – ♭♭7**

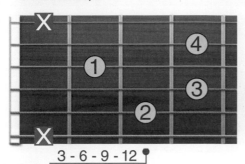

3 - 6 - 9 - 12

Cdim5

Alternate Names
C diminished fifth, C–5, C(♭5)

Chord Notes   **C – E – G♭**
Chord Formula **1 – 3 – ♭5**

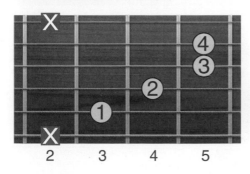

2   3   4   5

Cdim5

Alternate Names
C diminished fifth, C–5, C(♭5)

Chord Notes   **C – E – G♭**
Chord Formula **1 – 3 – ♭5**

7   8   9   10

C

C7aug5

Alternate Names
C seventh augmented fifth, C7+5, C7#5

Chord Notes   **C – E – G# – B♭**
Chord Formula   **1 – 3 – #5 – ♭7**

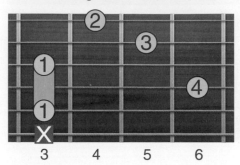

C7dim5

Alternate Names
C seventh diminished fifth, C7–5, C7♭5

Chord Notes   **C – E – G♭ – B♭**
Chord Formula   **1 – 3 – ♭5 – ♭7**

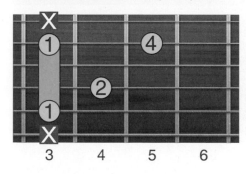

C7aug9

Alternate Names
C seventh augmented ninth, C7+9, C7#9

Chord Notes   **C – E – G – B♭ – D#**
Chord Formula   **1 – 3 – 5 – ♭7 – #9**

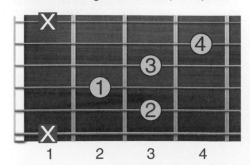

C7dim9

Alternate Names
C seventh diminished ninth, C7–9, C7♭9

Chord Notes   **C – E – G – B♭ – D♭**
Chord Formula   **1 – 3 – 5 – ♭7 – ♭9**

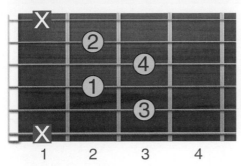

1   2   3   4

C11

Alternate Names
C eleventh

Chord Notes   **C – E – G – B♭ – D – F**
Chord Formula   **1 – 3 – 5 – ♭7 – 9 – 11**

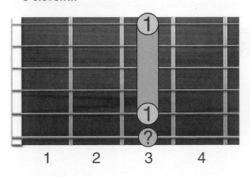

1   2   3   4

C13

Alternate Names
C thirteenth

Chord Notes   **C – E – G – B♭ – D – A**
Chord Formula   **1 – 3 – 5 – ♭7 – 9 – 13**

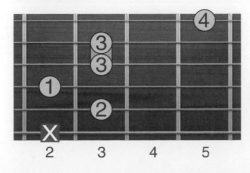

2   3   4   5

Music in the Key of C

Better Be Home Soon – Crowded House

No Woman, No Cry – Bob Marley

Imagine – John Lennon

Jackson – Johnny Cash

Let it Be – The Beatles

Symphony No. 5 in C minor – Ludwig van Beethoven

Wedding March – Felix Mendelssohn

C♯ D♭

The C♯ major scale consists of seven sharps: C♯, D♯, E♯ (for which you play an F), F♯, G♯, A♯ and B♯ (for which you play a C). In this section of the chord dictionary, E♯ is represented as F and B♯ is represented as C for simplicity.

The C♯ minor scale consists of four sharps: C♯, D♯, F♯ and G♯.

The D♭ major scale consists of five flats: D♭, E♭, G♭, A♭ and B♭.

The D♭ minor scale consists of seven flats and one double flat: D♭, E♭, F♭ (for which you play an E), G♭, A♭, B♭♭ (for which you play an A) and C♭ (for which you play a B).

The minor flavour of this key makes it especially well suited to funk, electric blues and metal. This key can sound soulful and uplifting, but with a touch of struggle and pathos.

The relative minor for C♯ major is A♯ minor.

The relative minor for D♭ major is B♭ minor.

C♯ Major Scale							
C♯	D♯	E♯ (F)	F♯	G♯	A♯	B♯ (C)	C♯
I	II	III	IV	V	VI	VII	I
1st	2nd	3rd	4th	5th	6th	7th	8th
	9th		11th		13th		

A♯ Minor Scale (Natural Minor)							
A♯	B♯ (C)	C♯	D♯	E♯ (F)	F♯	G♯	A♯
I	II	III	IV	V	VI	VII	I
1st	2nd	♭3rd	4th	5th	♭6th	♭7th	8th
	9th		11th		13th		

C#

Alternate Names
C# major, C#maj, C#M

Chord Notes   **C# – F – G#**
Chord Formula   **1 – 3 – 5**

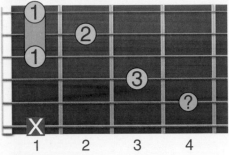

C#

Alternate Names
C# major, C#maj, C#M

Chord Notes   **C# – F – G#**
Chord Formula   **1 – 3 – 5**

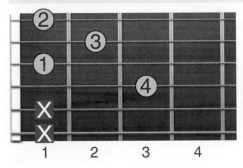

C#

Alternate Names
C# major, C#maj, C#M

Chord Notes   **C# – F – G#**
Chord Formula   **1 – 3 – 5**

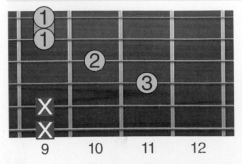

C#7

Alternate Names
C# seventh, C#dom7

Chord Notes   **C# – F – G# – B**
Chord Formula   **1 – 3 – 5 – ♭7**

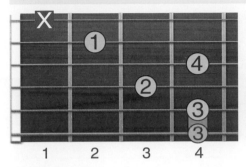

1   2   3   4

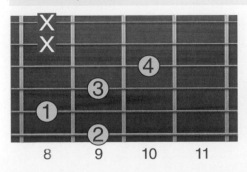

C#7

Alternate Names
C# seventh, C#dom7

Chord Notes   **C# – F – G# – B**
Chord Formula   **1 – 3 – 5 – ♭7**

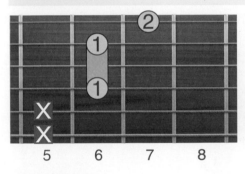

5   6   7   8

C#7

Alternate Names
C# seventh, C#dom7

Chord Notes   **C# – F – G# – B**
Chord Formula   **1 – 3 – 5 – ♭7**

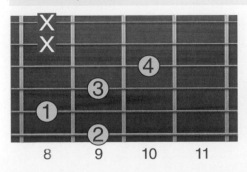

8   9   10   11

C#m

Alternate Names
C# minor, C#min, C#–

Chord Notes   C# – E – G#
Chord Formula 1 – ♭3 – 5

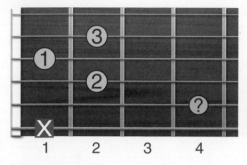

1   2   3   4

C#m

Alternate Names
C# minor, C#min, C#–

Chord Notes   C# – E – G#
Chord Formula 1 – ♭3 – 5

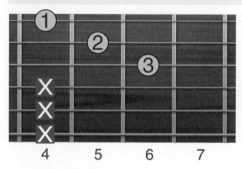

4   5   6   7

C#m

Alternate Names
C# minor, C#min, C#–

Chord Notes   C# – E – G#
Chord Formula 1 – ♭3 – 5

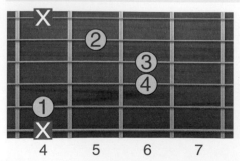

4   5   6   7

C#m7

Alternate Names
C#minor7, C#min7, C#–7

Chord Notes   **C# – E – G# – B**
Chord Formula   **1 – ♭3 – 5 – ♭7**

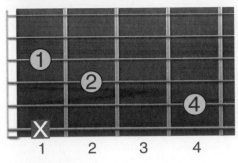

1   2   3   4

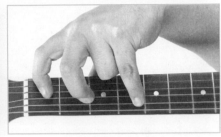

C#m7

Alternate Names
C#minor7, C#min7, C#–7

Chord Notes   **C# – E – G# – B**
Chord Formula   **1 – ♭3 – 5 – ♭7**

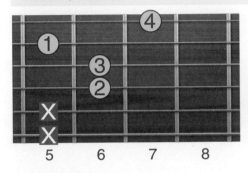

5   6   7   8

C#m7

Alternate Names
C#minor7, C#min7, C#–7

Chord Notes   **C# – E – G# – B**
Chord Formula   **1 – ♭3 – 5 – ♭7**

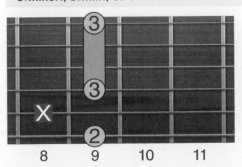

8   9   10   11

C#maj7

Alternate Names
C# Major7, C#M7, C#Δ7

Chord Notes   **C# – F – G# – C**
Chord Formula   **1 – 3 – 5 – 7**

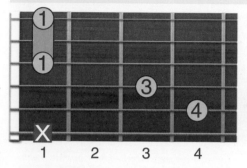

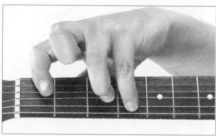

| 1 | 2 | 3 | 4 |

C#maj7

Alternate Names
C# Major7, C#M7, C#Δ7

Chord Notes   **C# – F – G# – C**
Chord Formula   **1 – 3 – 5 – 7**

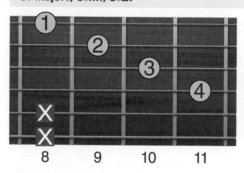

| 8 | 9 | 10 | 11 |

C#sus2

Alternate Names
C# suspended second

Chord Notes   **C# – D# – G#**
Chord Formula   **1 – 2 – 5**

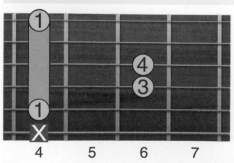

| 4 | 5 | 6 | 7 |

C#sus2

Alternate Names
C# suspended second

Chord Notes   **C# – D# – G#**
Chord Formula   **1 – 2 – 5**

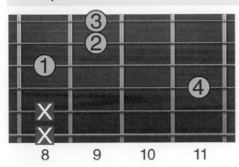

8   9   10   11

C#sus4

Alternate Names
C# suspended fourth

Chord Notes   **C# – F# – G#**
Chord Formula   **1 – 4 – 5**

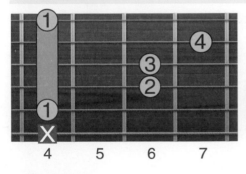

4   5   6   7

C#sus4

Alternate Names
C# suspended fourth

Chord Notes   **C# – F# – G#**
Chord Formula   **1 – 4 – 5**

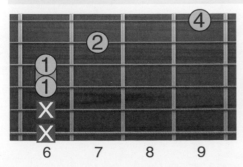

6   7   8   9

C#
D♭

C#7sus4

Alternate Names
C#7 suspended fourth

Chord Notes   **C# – F# – G# – B**
Chord Formula   **1 – 4 – 5 – ♭7**

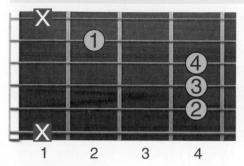

1   2   3   4

C#7sus4

Alternate Names
C#7 suspended fourth

Chord Notes   **C# – F# – G# – B**
Chord Formula   **1 – 4 – 5 – ♭7**

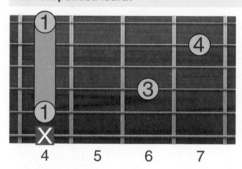

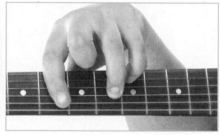

4   5   6   7

C#6

Alternate Names
C# sixth, C# major 6, C#maj6, C#M6

Chord Notes   **C# – F – G# – A#**
Chord Formula   **1 – 3 – 5 – 6**

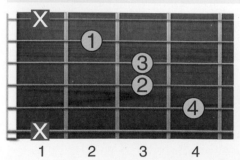

1   2   3   4

C#6

Alternate Names
C# sixth, C# major 6, C#maj6, C#M6

Chord Notes **C# – F – G# – A#**
Chord Formula **1 – 3 – 5 – 6**

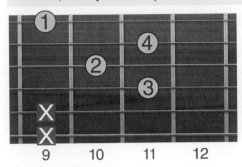
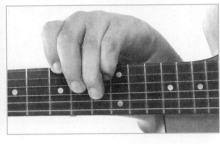

9   10   11   12

C#m6

Alternate Names
C# minor sixth, C#min6

Chord Notes **C# – E – G# – A#**
Chord Formula **1 – ♭3 – 5 – 6**

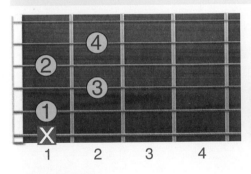
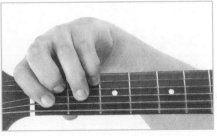

1   2   3   4

C#m6

Alternate Names
C# minor sixth, C#min6

Chord Notes **C# – E – G# – A#**
Chord Formula **1 – ♭3 – 5 – 6**

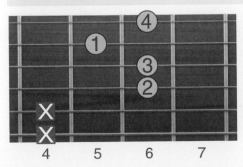

4   5   6   7

85

C#9

Alternate Names
C# ninth, C#dom9

Chord Notes   **C# – F – G# – B – D#**
Chord Formula   **1 – 3 – 5 – b7 – 9**

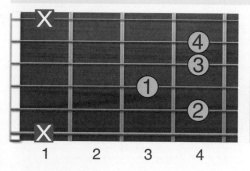

1   2   3   4

C#9

Alternate Names
C# ninth, C#dom9

Chord Notes   **C# – F – G# – B – D#**
Chord Formula   **1 – 3 – 5 – b7 – 9**

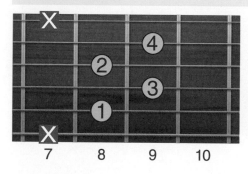

7   8   9   10

C#maj9

Alternate Names
C# major ninth, C#M9, C#Δ9

Chord Notes   **C# – F – G# – C – D#**
Chord Formula   **1 – 3 – 5 – 7 – 9**

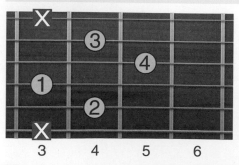

3   4   5   6

C#m9

Alternate Names
C# minor ninth, C#min9

Chord Notes   C# – E – G# – B – D#
Chord Formula   1 – ♭3 – 5 – ♭7 – 9

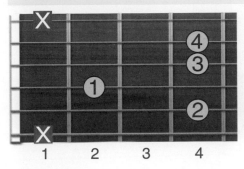

1   2   3   4

C#
D♭

C#m9

Alternate Names
C# minor ninth, C#min9

Chord Notes   C# – E – G# – B – D#
Chord Formula   1 – ♭3 – 5 – ♭7 – 9

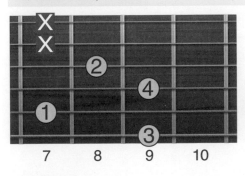

7   8   9   10

C#6/9

Alternate Names
C# six nine, C# major sixth added 9

Chord Notes   C# – F – G# – A# – D#
Chord Formula   1 – 3 – 5 – 6 – 9

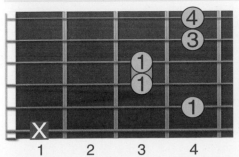

1   2   3   4

C#aug

Alternate Names
C# augmented, C#+

Chord Notes   **C# – F – A**
Chord Formula   **1 – 3 – #5**

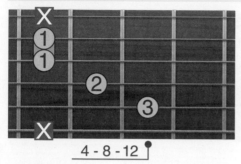

4 - 8 - 12

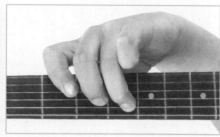

C#aug

Alternate Names
C# augmented, C#+

Chord Notes   **C# – F – A**
Chord Formula   **1 – 3 – #5**

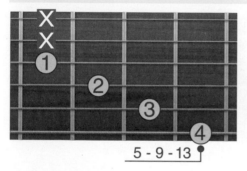

5 - 9 - 13

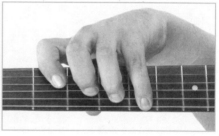

C#dim

Alternate Names
C# diminished, C#°

Chord Notes   **C# – E – G – B♭**
Chord Formula   **1 – ♭3 – ♭5 – ♭♭7**

3 - 6 - 9 - 12

C#
D♭

C#dim

Alternate Names
C# diminished, C#°

Chord Notes   **C# – E – G – B♭**
Chord Formula   **1 – ♭3 – ♭5 – ♭♭7**

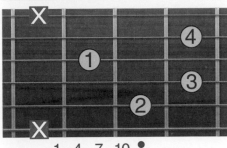

1 - 4 - 7 - 10

C#dim5

Alternate Names
C# diminished fifth, C#–5, C#(♭5)

Chord Notes   **C# – F – G**
Chord Formula   **1 – 3 – ♭5**

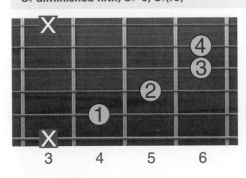

3   4   5   6

C#dim5

Alternate Names
C# diminished fifth, C#–5, C#(♭5)

Chord Notes   **C# – F – G**
Chord Formula   **1 – 3 – ♭5**

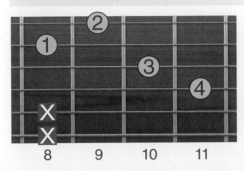

8   9   10   11

C#
D♭

89

C#7aug5

Alternate Names
C# seventh augmented fifth, C#7+5, C#7#5

Chord Notes   **C# – F – A – B**
Chord Formula **1 – 3 – #5 – ♭7**

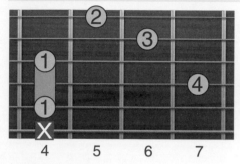

4   5   6   7

C#7dim5

Alternate Names
C# seventh diminished fifth, C#7–5, C#7♭5

Chord Notes   **C# – F – G – B**
Chord Formula **1 – 3 – ♭5 – ♭7**

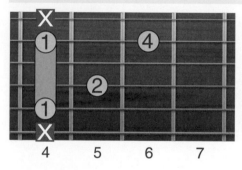

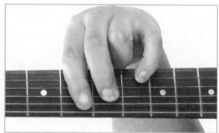

4   5   6   7

C#7aug9

Alternate Names
C# seventh augmented ninth, C#7+9, C#7#9

Chord Notes   **C# – F – G# – B – E**
Chord Formula **1 – 3 – 5 – ♭7 – #9**

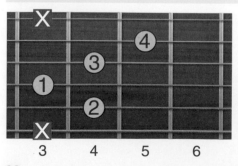

3   4   5   6

C#7dim9

Alternate Names
C# seventh diminished ninth, C#7–9, C#7♭9

Chord Notes **C# – F – G# – B – D**
Chord Formula **1 – 3 – 5 – ♭7 – ♭9**

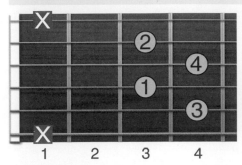

1   2   3   4

C#11

Alternate Names
C# eleventh

Chord Notes **C# – F – G# – B – D# – F#**
Chord Formula **1 – 3 – 5 – ♭7 – 9 – 11**

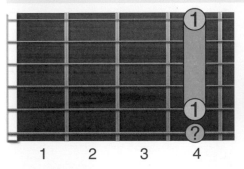

1   2   3   4

C#13

Alternate Names
C# thirteenth

Chord Notes **C# – F – G# – B – D# – A#**
Chord Formula **1 – 3 – 5 – ♭7 – 9 – 13**

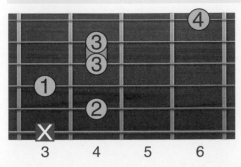

3   4   5   6

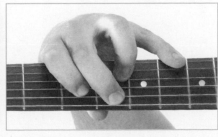

C#
D♭

Music in the Key of C♯/D♭

All Torn Down – The Living End

Lullaby – The Cure

Mr. Brightside – The Killers

All Over You – Live

*Piano Sonata No. 14 in C-sharp minor
(Moonlight Sonata) – Ludwig van Beethoven*

D

The D major scale consists of two sharps: F♯ and C♯.

The D minor scale consists of one flat: B♭.

Popular for folk, pop and country music, D major is one of the happiest-sounding keys while D minor is one of the saddest. Lowering the 6th string of the guitar down a whole step gives you a drop D tuning, which is popular in grunge, metal and blues.

The relative minor for D major is B minor.

D Major Scale							
D	E	F♯	G	A	B	C♯	D
I	II	III	IV	V	VI	VII	I
1st	2nd	3rd	4th	5th	6th	7th	8th
	9th		11th		13th		

B Minor Scale (Natural Minor)							
B	C♯	D	E	F♯	G	A	B
I	II	III	IV	V	VI	VII	I
1st	2nd	♭3rd	4th	5th	♭6th	♭7th	8th
	9th		11th		13th		

D

Alternate Names
D major, Dmaj, DM

Chord Notes   **D – F♯ – A**
Chord Formula   **1 – 3 – 5**

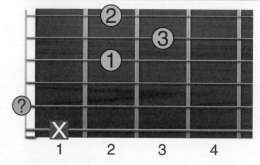

1   2   3   4

D

Alternate Names
D major, Dmaj, DM

Chord Notes   **D – F♯ – A**
Chord Formula   **1 – 3 – 5**

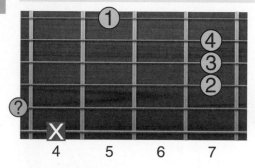

4   5   6   7

D

Alternate Names
D major, Dmaj, DM

Chord Notes   **D – F♯ – A**
Chord Formula   **1 – 3 – 5**

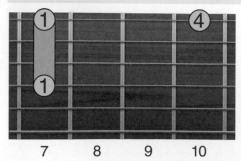
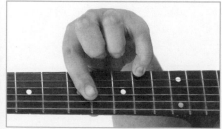

7   8   9   10

94

D7

Alternate Names
D seventh, Ddom7

Chord Notes **D – F# – A – C**
Chord Formula **1 – 3 – 5 – ♭7**

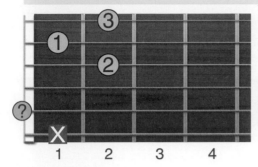

D7

Alternate Names
D seventh, Ddom7

Chord Notes **D – F# – A – C**
Chord Formula **1 – 3 – 5 – ♭7**

D

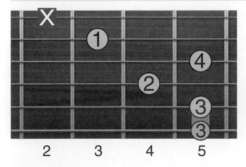

D7

Alternate Names
D seventh, Ddom7

Chord Notes **D – F# – A – C**
Chord Formula **1 – 3 – 5 – ♭7**

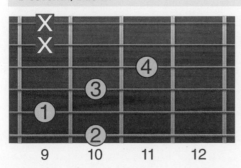

Dm

Alternate Names
D minor, Dmin, D–

Chord Notes   **D – F – A**
Chord Formula   **1 – ♭3 – 5**

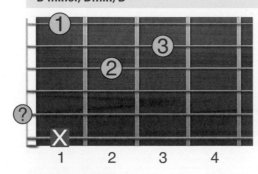

1   2   3   4

Dm

Alternate Names
D minor, Dmin, D–

Chord Notes   **D – F – A**
Chord Formula   **1 – ♭3 – 5**

5   6   7   8

Dm

Alternate Names
D minor, Dmin, D–

Chord Notes   **D – F – A**
Chord Formula   **1 – ♭3 – 5**

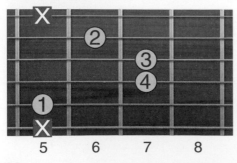

5   6   7   8

D

96

Dm7

Alternate Names
Dminor7, Dmin7, D–7

Chord Notes **D – F – A – C**
Chord Formula **1 – ♭3 – 5 – ♭7**

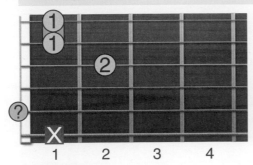

Dm7

Alternate Names
Dminor7, Dmin7, D–7

Chord Notes **D – F – A – C**
Chord Formula **1 – ♭3 – 5 – ♭7**

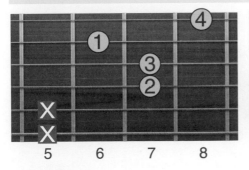

Dm7

Alternate Names
Dminor7, Dmin7, D–7

Chord Notes **D – F – A – C**
Chord Formula **1 – ♭3 – 5 – ♭7**

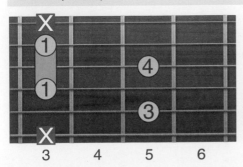

D

Dmaj7

Alternate Names
D Major7, DM7, DΔ7

Chord Notes   **D – F# – A – C#**
Chord Formula   **1 – 3 – 5 – 7**

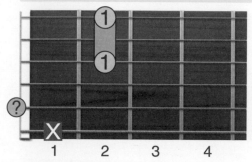

     1   2   3   4

Dmaj7

Alternate Names
D Major7, DM7, DΔ7

Chord Notes   **D – F# – A – C#**
Chord Formula   **1 – 3 – 5 – 7**

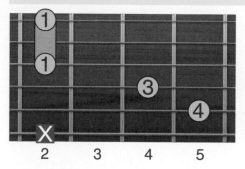

     2   3   4   5

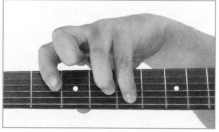

Dsus2

Alternate Names
D suspended second

Chord Notes   **D – E – A**
Chord Formula   **1 – 2 – 5**

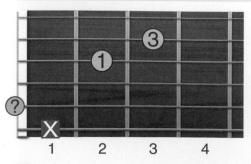

     1   2   3   4

D

Dsus2

Alternate Names
D suspended second

Chord Notes **D – E – A**
Chord Formula **1 – 2 – 5**

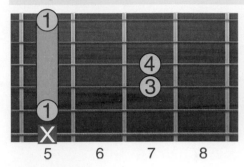
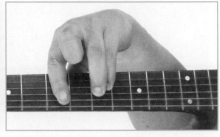

5   6   7   8

Dsus4

Alternate Names
D suspended fourth

Chord Notes **D – G – A**
Chord Formula **1 – 4 – 5**

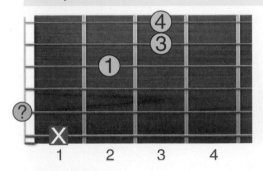

1   2   3   4

D

Dsus4

Alternate Names
D suspended fourth

Chord Notes **D – G – A**
Chord Formula **1 – 4 – 5**

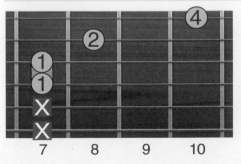

7   8   9   10

D7sus4

Alternate Names
D7 suspended fourth

Chord Notes   **D – G – A – C**
Chord Formula   **1 – 4 – 5 – ♭7**

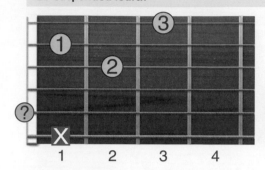

D7sus4

Alternate Names
D7 suspended fourth

Chord Notes   **D – G – A – C**
Chord Formula   **1 – 4 – 5 – ♭7**

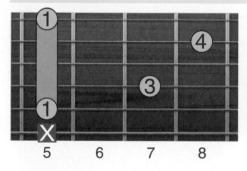
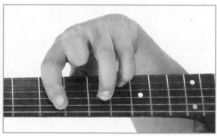

D6

Alternate Names
D sixth, D major 6, Dmaj6, DM6

Chord Notes   **D – F♯ – A – B**
Chord Formula   **1 – 3 – 5 – 6**

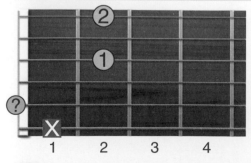

100

D6

Alternate Names
D sixth, D major 6, Dmaj6, DM6

Chord Notes   **D – F# – A – B**
Chord Formula   **1 – 3 – 5 – 6**

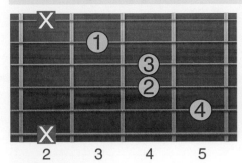

2   3   4   5

Dm6

Alternate Names
D minor sixth, Dmin6

Chord Notes   **D – F – A – B**
Chord Formula   **1 – ♭3 – 5 – 6**

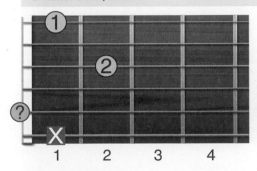

1   2   3   4

Dm6

Alternate Names
D minor sixth, Dmin6

Chord Notes   **D – F – A – B**
Chord Formula   **1 – ♭3 – 5 – 6**

5   6   7   8

D9

Alternate Names
D ninth, Ddom9

Chord Notes   **D – F♯ – A – C – E**
Chord Formula   **1 – 3 – 5 – ♭7 – 9**

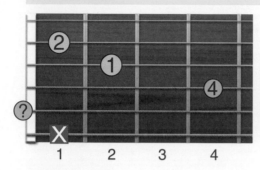

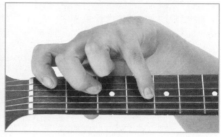

1   2   3   4

D

D9

Alternate Names
D ninth, Ddom9

Chord Notes   **D – F♯ – A – C – E**
Chord Formula   **1 – 3 – 5 – ♭7 – 9**

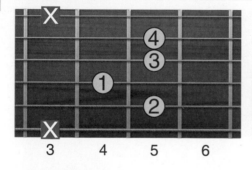

3   4   5   6

Dmaj9

Alternate Names
D major ninth, DM9, DΔ9

Chord Notes   **D – F♯ – A – C♯ – E**
Chord Formula   **1 – 3 – 5 – 7 – 9**

1   2   3   4

102

Dm9

Alternate Names
D minor ninth, Dmin9, D–9

Chord Notes   **D – F – A – C – E**
Chord Formula   **1 – ♭3 – 5 – ♭7 – 9**

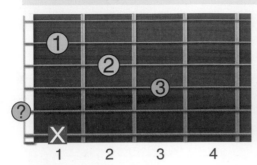

Dm9

Alternate Names
D minor ninth, Dmin9, D–9

Chord Notes   **D – F – A – C – E**
Chord Formula   **1 – ♭3 – 5 – ♭7 – 9**

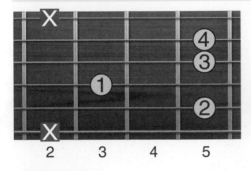

D6/9

Alternate Names
D six nine, D major sixth added 9

Chord Notes   **D – F♯ – A – B – E**
Chord Formula   **1 – 3 – 5 – 6 – 9**

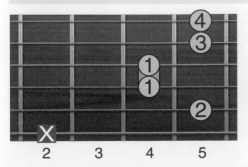

Daug

Alternate Names
D augmented, D+

Chord Notes   **D – F♯ – A♯**
Chord Formula **1 – 3 – ♯5**

5 - 9 - 13

D

Daug

Alternate Names
D augmented, D+

Chord Notes   **D – F♯ – A♯**
Chord Formula **1 – 3 – ♯5**

6 - 10 - 14

Ddim

Alternate Names
D diminished, D°

Chord Notes   **D – F – G♯ – B**
Chord Formula **1 – ♭3 – ♭5 – ♭♭7**

1 - 4 - 7 - 10

Ddim

Alternate Names
D diminished, D°

Chord Notes   **D – F – A♭ – C♭**
Chord Formula   **1 – ♭3 – ♭5 – ♭♭7**

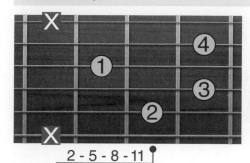

2 - 5 - 8 - 11

Ddim5

Alternate Names
D diminished fifth, D–5, D(♭5)

Chord Notes   **D – F♯ – A♭**
Chord Formula   **1 – 3 – ♭5**

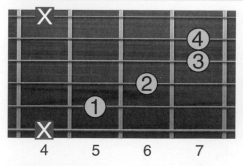

4   5   6   7

D

Ddim5

Alternate Names
D diminished fifth, D–5, D(♭5)

Chord Notes   **D – F♯ – A♭**
Chord Formula   **1 – 3 – ♭5**

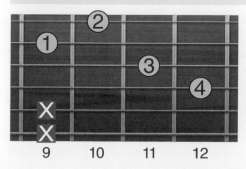

9   10   11   12

D7aug5

Alternate Names
D seventh augmented fifth, D7+5, D7♯5

Chord Notes   **D – F♯ – A♯ – C**
Chord Formula   **1 – 3 – ♯5 – ♭7**

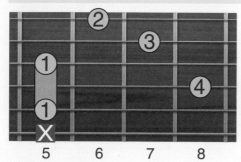

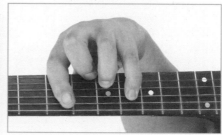

5   6   7   8

D7dim5

Alternate Names
D seventh diminished fifth, D7–5, D7♭5

Chord Notes   **D – F♯ – A♭ – C**
Chord Formula   **1 – 3 – ♭5 – ♭7**

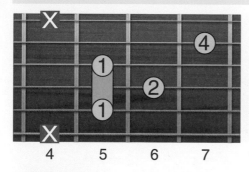

4   5   6   7

D7aug9

Alternate Names
D seventh augmented ninth, D7+9, D7♯9

Chord Notes   **D – F♯ – A – C – F**
Chord Formula   **1 – 3 – 5 – ♭7 – ♯9**

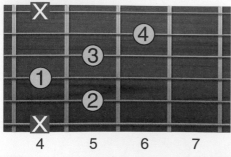

4   5   6   7

D7dim9

Alternate Names
D seventh diminished ninth, D7–9, D7♭9

Chord Notes   D – F♯ – A – C – E♭
Chord Formula   1 – 3 – 5 – ♭7 – ♭9

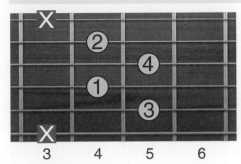

3   4   5   6

D11

Alternate Names
D eleventh

Chord Notes   D – F♯ – A – C – E – G
Chord Formula   1 – 3 – 5 – ♭7 – 9 – 11

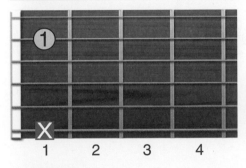

1   2   3   4

D

D13

Alternate Names
D thirteenth

Chord Notes   D – F♯ – A – C – E – B
Chord Formula   1 – 3 – 5 – ♭7 – 9 – 13

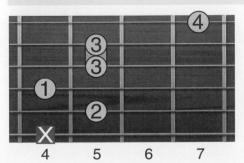

4   5   6   7

Music in the Key of D

Layla – Eric Clapton

Mother Nature's Son – The Beatles

Another Brick in the Wall – Pink Floyd

Summer of '69 – Bryan Adams

Like the Way I Do – Melissa Etheridge

Canon in D major (Pachelbel's Canon) – Johann Pachelbel

Hallelujah Chorus from Messiah – George Frideric Handel

D♯ E♭

The E♭ major scale consists of three flats: E♭, A♭ and B♭.

The E♭ minor scale consists of six flats: E♭, G♭, A♭, B♭, C♭ (for which you play a B) and D♭.

The D♯ major scale is rarely used in music, as it has so many sharpened notes that it is easier to refer to the E♭ major scale.

The D♯ minor scale consists of six sharps: D♯, E♯ (for which you play an F), F♯, G♯, A♯ and C♯.

E♭ major is a good key for jazz and accompanying brass instruments. Many blues guitarists tune their whole guitar down half a step to play in this key. E♭ minor is favoured by neo-classical guitarists such as Yngwie Malmsteen. It has been said to sound dark and mysterious.

The relative minor for E♭ major is C minor.

E♭ Major Scale

E♭	F	G	A♭	B♭	C	D	E♭
I	II	III	IV	V	VI	VII	I
1st	2nd	3rd	4th	5th	6th	7th	8th
	9th		11th		13th		

C Minor Scale (Natural Minor)

C	D	E♭	F	G	A♭	B♭	C
I	II	III	IV	V	VI	VII	I
1st	2nd	♭3rd	4th	5th	♭6th	♭7th	8th
	9th		11th		13th		

E♭

Alternate Names
E♭ major, E♭maj, E♭M

Chord Notes   **E♭ – G – B♭**
Chord Formula   **1 – 3 – 5**

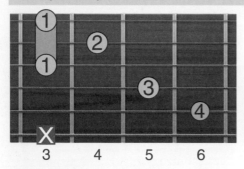

    3   4   5   6

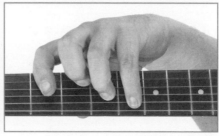

E♭

Alternate Names
E♭ major, E♭maj, E♭M

Chord Notes   **E♭ – G – B♭**
Chord Formula   **1 – 3 – 5**

    3   4   5   6

E♭

Alternate Names
E♭ major, E♭maj, E♭M

Chord Notes   **E♭ – G – B♭**
Chord Formula   **1 – 3 – 5**

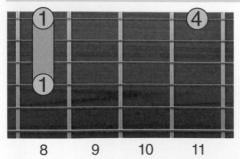

    8   9   10   11

D#
E♭

E♭7

Alternate Names
E♭ seventh, E♭dom7

Chord Notes   E♭ – G – B♭ – D♭
Chord Formula   1 – 3 – 5 – ♭7

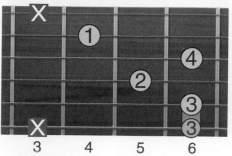

3   4   5   6

E♭7

Alternate Names
E♭ seventh, E♭dom7

Chord Notes   E♭ – G – B♭ – D♭
Chord Formula   1 – 3 – 5 – ♭7

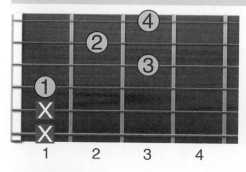

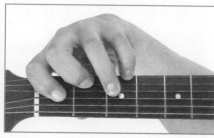

1   2   3   4

D♯
E♭

E♭7

Alternate Names
E♭ seventh, E♭dom7

Chord Notes   E♭ – G – B♭ – D♭
Chord Formula   1 – 3 – 5 – ♭7

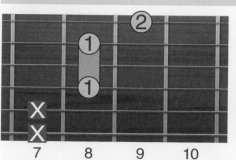

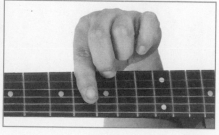

7   8   9   10

111

E♭m

Alternate Names
E♭ minor, E♭min, E♭–

Chord Notes   E♭ – G♭ – B♭
Chord Formula   **1 – ♭3 – 5**

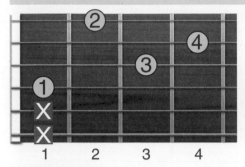

1   2   3   4

E♭m

Alternate Names
E♭ minor, E♭min, E♭–

Chord Notes   E♭ – G♭ – B♭
Chord Formula   **1 – ♭3 – 5**

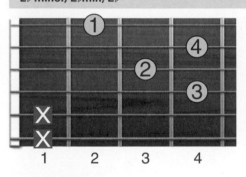

1   2   3   4

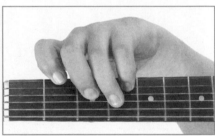

E♭m

Alternate Names
E♭ minor, E♭min, E♭–

Chord Notes   E♭ – G♭ – B♭
Chord Formula   **1 – ♭3 – 5**

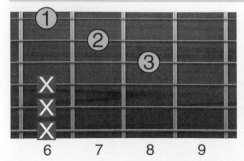

6   7   8   9

E♭m7

Alternate Names
E♭minor7, E♭min7, E♭–7

Chord Notes   E♭ – G♭ – B♭ – D♭
Chord Formula   1 – ♭3 – 5 – ♭7

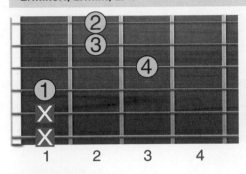

1   2   3   4

E♭m7

Alternate Names
E♭minor7, E♭min7, E♭–7

Chord Notes   E♭ – G♭ – B♭ – D♭
Chord Formula   1 – ♭3 – 5 – ♭7

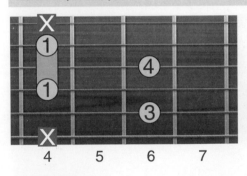

4   5   6   7

D#
E♭

E♭m7

Alternate Names
E♭minor7, E♭min7, E♭–7

Chord Notes   E♭ – G♭ – B♭ – D♭
Chord Formula   1 – ♭3 – 5 – ♭7

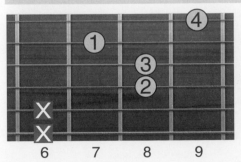

6   7   8   9

E♭maj7

Alternate Names
E♭ Major7, E♭M7, E♭Δ7

Chord Notes   E♭ – G – B♭ – D
Chord Formula 1 – 3 – 5 – 7

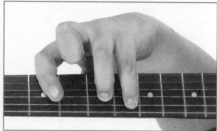

3   4   5   6

E♭maj7

Alternate Names
E♭ Major7, E♭M7, E♭Δ7

Chord Notes   E♭ – G – B♭ – D
Chord Formula 1 – 3 – 5 – 7

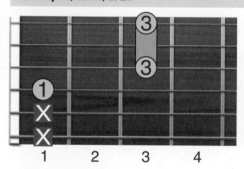

1   2   3   4

E♭sus2

Alternate Names
E♭ suspended second

Chord Notes   E♭ – F – B♭
Chord Formula 1 – 2 – 5

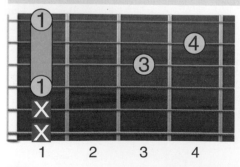
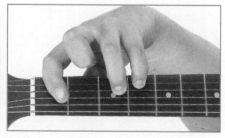

1   2   3   4

D#
E♭

E♭sus2

Alternate Names
E♭ suspended second

Chord Notes   **E♭ – F – B♭**
Chord Formula   **1 – 2 – 5**

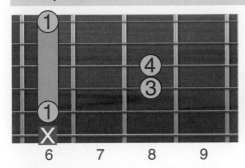
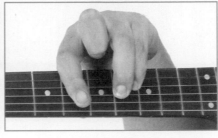

E♭sus4

Alternate Names
E♭ suspended fourth

Chord Notes   **E♭ – A♭ – B♭**
Chord Formula   **1 – 4 – 5**

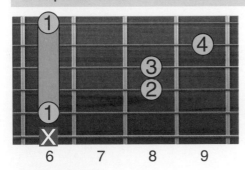
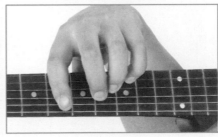

E♭sus4

Alternate Names
E♭ suspended fourth

Chord Notes   **E♭ – A♭ – B♭**
Chord Formula   **1 – 4 – 5**

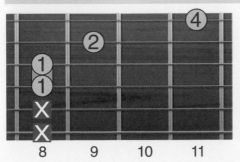

D#
E♭

115

Eb7sus4

Alternate Names
Eb7 suspended fourth

Chord Notes   Eb – Ab – Bb – Db
Chord Formula   1 – 4 – 5 – b7

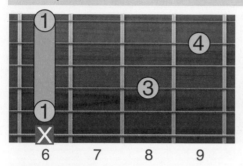

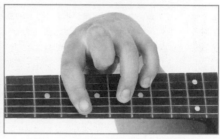

6   7   8   9

Eb7sus4

Alternate Names
Eb7 suspended fourth

Chord Notes   Eb – Ab – Bb – Db
Chord Formula   1 – 4 – 5 – b7

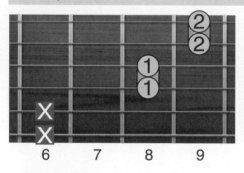

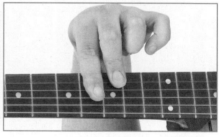

6   7   8   9

Eb6

Alternate Names
Eb sixth, Eb major 6, Ebmaj6, EbM6

Chord Notes   Eb – G – Bb – C
Chord Formula   1 – 3 – 5 – 6

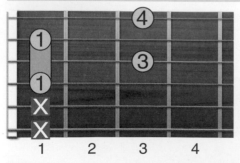

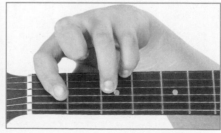

1   2   3   4

E♭6

Alternate Names
E♭ sixth, E♭ major 6, E♭maj6, E♭M6

Chord Notes   E♭ – G – B♭ – C
Chord Formula   1 – 3 – 5 – 6

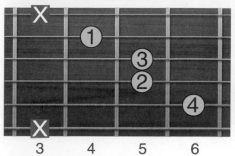

3   4   5   6

E♭m6

Alternate Names
E♭ minor sixth, E♭min6

Chord Notes   E♭ – G♭ – B♭ – C
Chord Formula   1 – ♭3 – 5 – 6

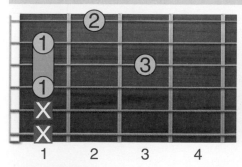

1   2   3   4

D#
E♭

E♭m6

Alternate Names
E♭ minor sixth, E♭min6

Chord Notes   E♭ – G♭ – B♭ – C
Chord Formula   1 – ♭3 – 5 – 6

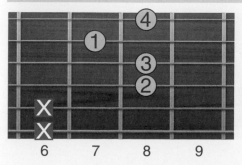

6   7   8   9

Eb9

Alternate Names
Eb ninth, Ebdom9

Chord Notes   **Eb – G – Bb – Db – F**
Chord Formula   **1 – 3 – 5 – b7 – 9**

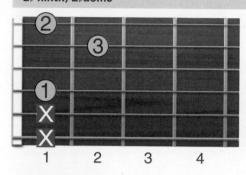

1   2   3   4

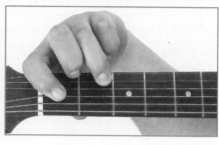

Eb9

Alternate Names
Eb ninth, Ebdom9

Chord Notes   **Eb – G – Bb – Db – F**
Chord Formula   **1 – 3 – 5 – b7 – 9**

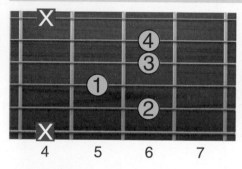

4   5   6   7

Ebmaj9

Alternate Names
Eb major ninth, EbM9, EbΔ9

Chord Notes   **Eb – G – Bb – D – F**
Chord Formula   **1 – 3 – 5 – 7 – 9**

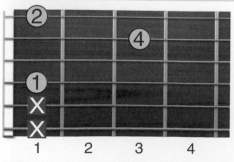

1   2   3   4

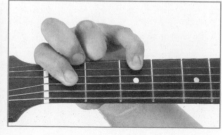

E♭m9

Alternate Names
E♭ minor ninth, E♭min9, E♭–9

Chord Notes   E♭ – G♭ – B♭ – D♭ – F
Chord Formula   1 – ♭3 – 5 – ♭7 – 9

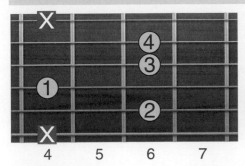
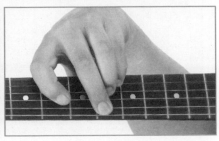

4   5   6   7

E♭m9

Alternate Names
E♭ minor ninth, E♭min9, E♭–9

Chord Notes   E♭ – G♭ – B♭ – D♭ – F
Chord Formula   1 – ♭3 – 5 – ♭7 – 9

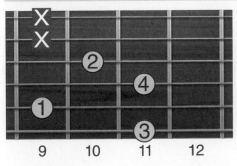
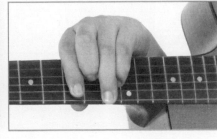

9   10   11   12

E♭6/9

Alternate Names
E♭ six nine, E♭ major sixth added 9

Chord Notes   E♭ – G – B♭ – C – F
Chord Formula   1 – 3 – 5 – 6 – 9

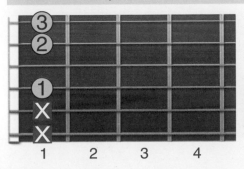

1   2   3   4

D♯
E♭

119

E♭aug

Alternate Names
E♭ augmented, E♭+

Chord Notes   **E♭ – G – B**
Chord Formula **1 – 3 – #5**

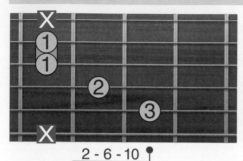

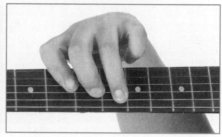

2 - 6 - 10

E♭aug

Alternate Names
E♭ augmented, E♭+

Chord Notes   **E♭ – G – B**
Chord Formula **1 – 3 – #5**

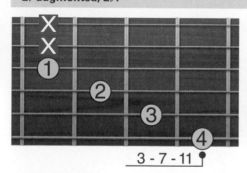

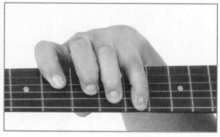

3 - 7 - 11

E♭dim

Alternate Names
E♭ diminished, E♭°

Chord Notes   **E♭ – G♭ – A – C**
Chord Formula **1 – ♭3 – ♭5 – ♭♭7**

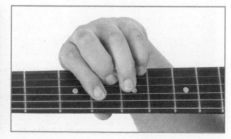

2 - 5 - 8 - 11

120

E♭dim

Alternate Names
E♭ diminished, E♭°

Chord Notes   **E♭ – G♭ – A – C**
Chord Formula   **1 – ♭3 – ♭5 – ♭♭7**

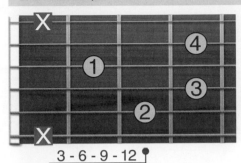

3 - 6 - 9 - 12

E♭dim5

Alternate Names
E♭ diminished fifth, E♭–5, E♭(♭5)

Chord Notes   **E♭ – G – A**
Chord Formula   **1 – 3 – ♭5**

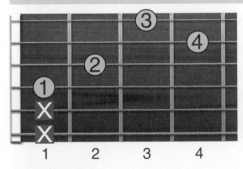

1   2   3   4

E♭dim5

Alternate Names
E♭ diminished fifth, E♭–5, E♭(♭5)

Chord Notes   **E♭ – G – A**
Chord Formula   **1 – 3 – ♭5**

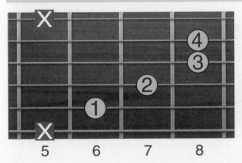

5   6   7   8

D#
E♭

Eb7aug5

Alternate Names
Eb seventh augmented fifth, Eb7+5, Eb7#5

Chord Notes   **Eb – G – B – Db**
Chord Formula   **1 – 3 – #5 – b7**

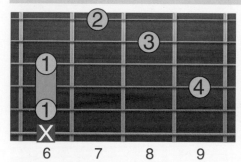

6   7   8   9

Eb7dim5

Alternate Names
Eb seventh diminished fifth, Eb7–5, Eb7b5

Chord Notes   **Eb – G – A – Db**
Chord Formula   **1 – 3 – b5 – b7**

D#
Eb

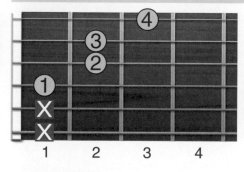

1   2   3   4

Eb7aug9

Alternate Names
Eb seventh augmented ninth, Eb7+9, Eb7#9

Chord Notes   **Eb – G – Bb – Db – F#**
Chord Formula   **1 – 3 – 5 – b7 – #9**

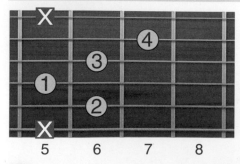

5   6   7   8

E♭7dim9

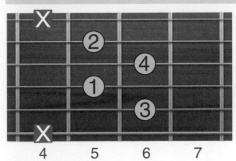

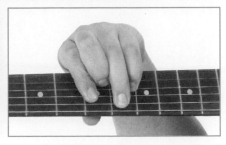

4   5   6   7

E♭11

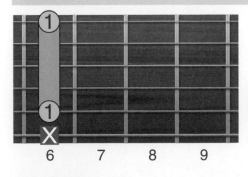

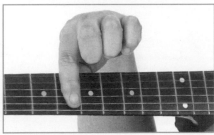

6   7   8   9

**D♯
E♭**

E♭13

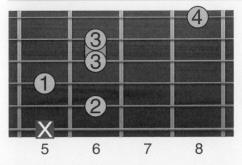

5   6   7   8

Music in the Key of D♯/E♭

Sober – Pink

Sledgehammer – Peter Gabriel

Lovely Rita – The Beatles

Superstition – Stevie Wonder

The Year 1812, Festival Overture in E flat major (The 1812 Overture) – Pyotr Ilyich Tchaikovsky

William Tell Overture – Gioachino Rossini

E

The E major scale consists of four sharps: F#, G#, C# and D#.

The E minor scale consists of one sharp: F#.

E is popular for blues, funk, rock, heavy metal and pretty much any other guitar-based genre. E minor is one of the best keys for guitarists due to the fact that it uses all the open strings (which are in the key of E minor).

The relative minor for E major is C# minor.

E Major Scale							
E	F#	G#	A	B	C#	D#	E
I	II	III	IV	V	VI	VII	I
1st	2nd	3rd	4th	5th	6th	7th	8th
	9th		11th		13th		

C# Minor Scale (Natural Minor)							
C#	D#	E	F#	G#	A	B	C#
I	II	III	IV	V	VI	VII	I
1st	2nd	b3rd	4th	5th	b6th	b7th	8th
	9th		11th		13th		

E

Alternate Names
E major, Emaj, EM

Chord Notes **E – G♯ – B**
Chord Formula **1 – 3 – 5**

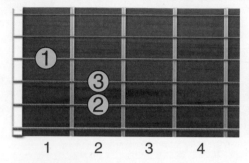

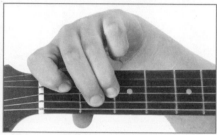

1   2   3   4

E

Alternate Names
E major, Emaj, EM

Chord Notes **E – G♯ – B**
Chord Formula **1 – 3 – 5**

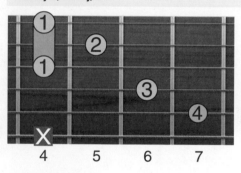

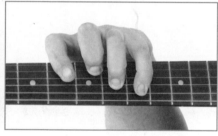

4   5   6   7

E

Alternate Names
E major, Emaj, EM

Chord Notes **E – G♯ – B**
Chord Formula **1 – 3 – 5**

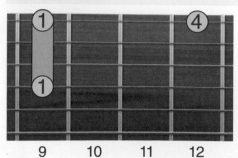

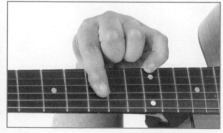

9   10   11   12

E7

Alternate Names
E seventh, Edom7

Chord Notes **E – G♯ – B – D**
Chord Formula **1 – 3 – 5 – ♭7**

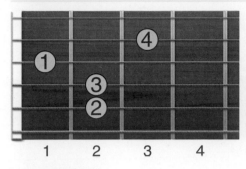

1   2   3   4

E7

Alternate Names
E seventh, Edom7

Chord Notes **E – G♯ – B – D**
Chord Formula **1 – 3 – 5 – ♭7**

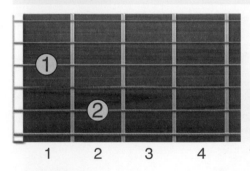

1   2   3   4

E7

Alternate Names
E seventh, Edom7

Chord Notes **E – G♯ – B – D**
Chord Formula **1 – 3 – 5 – ♭7**

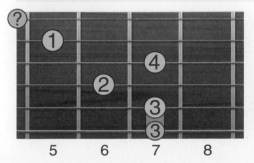

5   6   7   8

Em

Alternate Names
E minor, Emin, E–

Chord Notes **E – G – B**
Chord Formula **1 – ♭3 – 5**

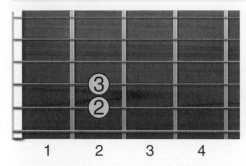

Em

Alternate Names
E minor, Emin, E–

Chord Notes **E – G – B**
Chord Formula **1 – ♭3 – 5**

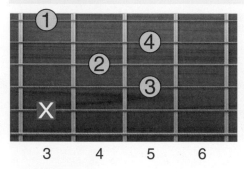

Em

Alternate Names
E minor, Emin, E–

Chord Notes **E – G – B**
Chord Formula **1 – ♭3 – 5**

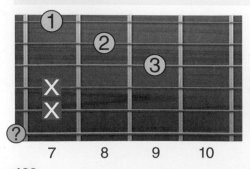

E

Em7

Alternate Names
Eminor7, Emin7, E–7

Chord Notes   **E – G – B – D**
Chord Formula   **1 – ♭3 – 5 – ♭7**

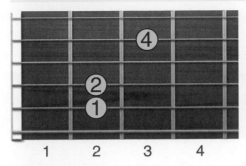

| 1 | 2 | 3 | 4 |

Em7

Alternate Names
Eminor7, Emin7, E–7

Chord Notes   **E – G – B – D**
Chord Formula   **1 – ♭3 – 5 – ♭7**

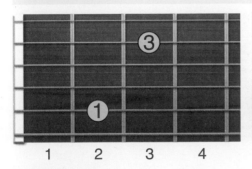

| 1 | 2 | 3 | 4 |

E

Em7

Alternate Names
Eminor7, Emin7, E–7

Chord Notes   **E – G – B – D**
Chord Formula   **1 – ♭3 – 5 – ♭7**

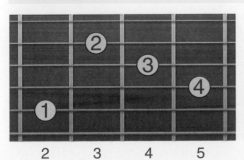

| 2 | 3 | 4 | 5 |

Emaj7

Alternate Names
E Major7, EM7, EΔ7

Chord Notes   **E – G# – B – D#**
Chord Formula **1 – 3 – 5 – 7**

1   2   3   4

Emaj7

Alternate Names
E Major7, EM7, EΔ7

Chord Notes   **E – G# – B – D#**
Chord Formula **1 – 3 – 5 – 7**

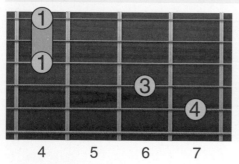

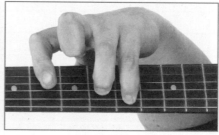

4   5   6   7

E

Esus2

Alternate Names
E suspended second

Chord Notes   **E – F# – B**
Chord Formula **1 – 2 – 5**

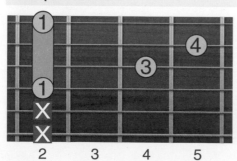

2   3   4   5

Esus2

Alternate Names
E suspended second

Chord Notes   **E – F♯ – B**
Chord Formula   **1 – 2 – 5**

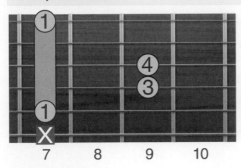

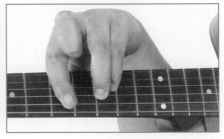

Esus4

Alternate Names
E suspended fourth

Chord Notes   **E – A – B**
Chord Formula   **1 – 4 – 5**

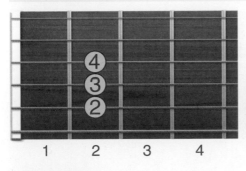

Esus4

Alternate Names
E suspended fourth

Chord Notes   **E – A – B**
Chord Formula   **1 – 4 – 5**

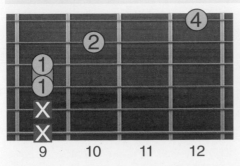

E

131

E7sus4

Alternate Names	Chord Notes	E – A – B – D
E7 suspended fourth	Chord Formula	**1 – 4 – 5 – ♭7**

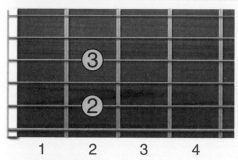 

1 2 3 4

E7sus4

Alternate Names	Chord Notes	E – A – B – D
E7 suspended fourth	Chord Formula	**1 – 4 – 5 – ♭7**

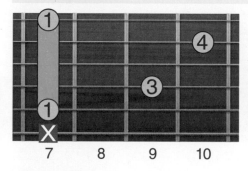 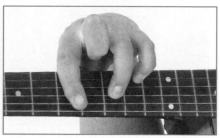

7 8 9 10

E

E6

Alternate Names	Chord Notes	E – G♯ – B – C♯
E sixth, E major 6, Emaj6, EM6	Chord Formula	**1 – 3 – 5 – 6**

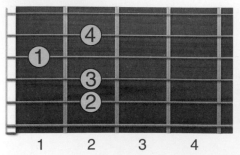 

1 2 3 4

E6

Alternate Names
E sixth, E major 6, Emaj6, EM6

Chord Notes   **E – G♯ – B – C♯**
Chord Formula **1 – 3 – 5 – 6**

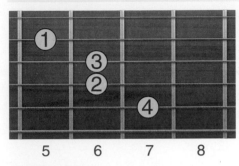

5   6   7   8

Em6

Alternate Names
E minor sixth, Emin6

Chord Notes   **E – G – B – C♯**
Chord Formula **1 – ♭3 – 5 – 6**

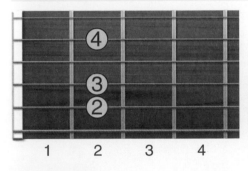

1   2   3   4

E

Em6

Alternate Names
E minor sixth, Emin6

Chord Notes   **E – G – B – C♯**
Chord Formula **1 – ♭3 – 5 – 6**

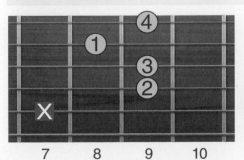

7   8   9   10

133

E9

Alternate Names
E ninth, Edom9

Chord Notes   E – G♯ – B – D – F♯
Chord Formula   1 – 3 – 5 – ♭7 – 9

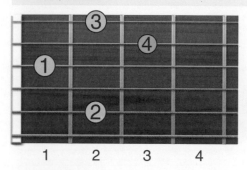

1   2   3   4

E9

Alternate Names
E ninth, Edom9

Chord Notes   E – G♯ – B – D – F♯
Chord Formula   1 – 3 – 5 – ♭7 – 9

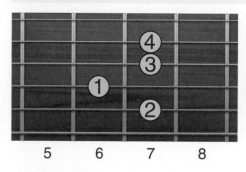

5   6   7   8

Emaj9

Alternate Names
E major ninth, EM9, E∆9

Chord Notes   E – G♯ – B – D♯ – F♯
Chord Formula   1 – 3 – 5 – 7 – 9

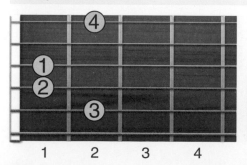

1   2   3   4

E

Em9

Alternate Names
E minor ninth, Emin9, E–9

Chord Notes **E – G – B – D – F♯**
Chord Formula **1 – ♭3 – 5 – ♭7 – 9**

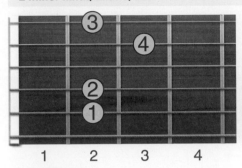

1   2   3   4

Em9

Alternate Names
E minor ninth, Emin9, E–9

Chord Notes **E – G – B – D – F♯**
Chord Formula **1 – ♭3 – 5 – ♭7 – 9**

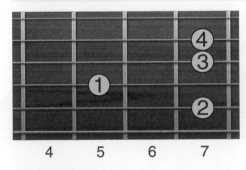

4   5   6   7

E

E6/9

Alternate Names
E six nine, E major sixth added 9

Chord Notes **E – G♯ – B – C♯ – F♯**
Chord Formula **1 – 3 – 5 – 6 – 9**

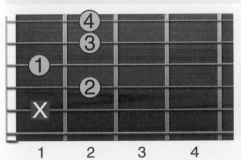

1   2   3   4

Eaug

Alternate Names
E augmented, E+

Chord Notes **E – G# – C**
Chord Formula **1 – 3 – #5**

1   2   3   4

Eaug

Alternate Names
E augmented, E+

Chord Notes **E – G# – C**
Chord Formula **1 – 3 – #5**

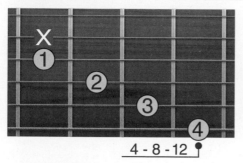

4 - 8 - 12

Edim

Alternate Names
E diminished, E°

Chord Notes **E – G – B♭ – D♭**
Chord Formula **1 – ♭3 – ♭5 – ♭♭7**

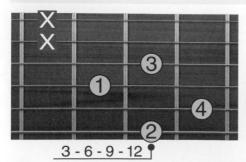

3 - 6 - 9 - 12

Edim

Alternate Names
E diminished, E°

Chord Notes   **E – G – B♭ – D♭**
Chord Formula   **1 – ♭3 – ♭5 – ♭♭7**

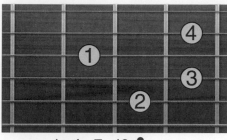

1 - 4 - 7 - 10

Edim5

Alternate Names
E diminished fifth, E–5, E(♭5)

Chord Notes   **E – G♯ – B♭**
Chord Formula   **1 – 3 – ♭5**

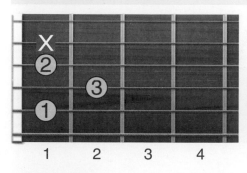

1   2   3   4

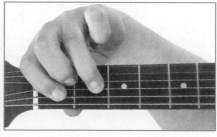

Edim5

Alternate Names
E diminished fifth, E–5, E(♭5)

Chord Notes   **E – G♯ – B♭**
Chord Formula   **1 – 3 – ♭5**

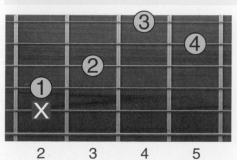

2   3   4   5

E

137

E7aug5

Alternate Names
E seventh augmented fifth, E7+5, E7♯5

Chord Notes   **E – G♯ – C – D**
Chord Formula   **1 – 3 – ♯5 – ♭7**

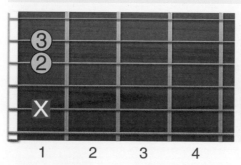

1   2   3   4

E7dim5

Alternate Names
E seventh diminished fifth, E7–5, E7♭5

Chord Notes   **E – G♯ – B♭ – D**
Chord Formula   **1 – 3 – ♭5 – ♭7**

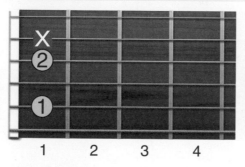

1   2   3   4

E7aug9

Alternate Names
E seventh augmented ninth, E7+9, E7♯9

Chord Notes   **E – G♯ – B – D – G**
Chord Formula   **1 – 3 – 5 – ♭7 – ♯9**

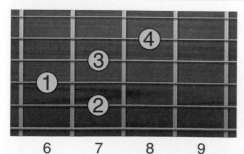

6   7   8   9

E

E7dim9

Alternate Names
E seventh diminished ninth, E7–9, E7♭9

Chord Notes **E – G♯ – B – D – F**
Chord Formula **1 – 3 – 5 – ♭7 – ♭9**

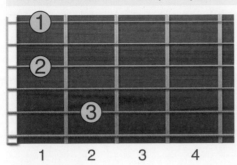 

1   2   3   4

E11

Alternate Names
E eleventh

Chord Notes **E – G♯ – B – D – F♯ – A**
Chord Formula **1 – 3 – 5 – ♭7 – 9 – 11**

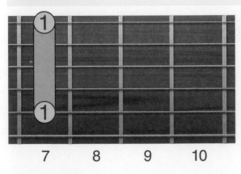 

7   8   9   10

E

E13

Alternate Names
E thirteenth

Chord Notes **E – G♯ – B – D – F♯ – C♯**
Chord Formula **1 – 3 – 5 – ♭7 – 9 – 13**

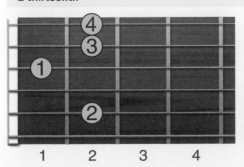 

1   2   3   4

Music in the Key of E

Little Wing – Jimi Hendrix

Back in Black – AC/DC

Please Please Me – The Beatles

Under the Bridge – Red Hot Chili Peppers

Enter Sandman – Metallica

Dance Of The Sugar-Plum Fairy, Nutcracker – Pyotr Ilyich Tchaikovsky

Concerto No. 1 in E major, La primavera (Spring) – Antonio Vivaldi

F

The F major scale consists of one flat: B♭.

The F minor scale consists of four flats: A♭, B♭, D♭ and E♭.

F major is a very pretty key that has been used effectively in a lot of ballads. It is also favoured by many classical composers and by brass and horn players, such as jazz musicians. F minor is a very passionate key, which is good for flamenco and Latin music.

The relative minor for F major is D minor.

F Major Scale							
F	G	A	B♭	C	D	E	F
I	II	III	IV	V	VI	VII	I
1st	2nd	3rd	4th	5th	6th	7th	8th
	9th		11th		13th		

D Minor Scale (Natural Minor)							
D	E	F	G	A	B♭	C	D
I	II	III	IV	V	VI	VII	I
1st	2nd	♭3rd	4th	5th	♭6th	♭7th	8th
	9th		11th		13th		

F

Alternate Names
F major, Fmaj, FM

Chord Notes   **F – A – C**
Chord Formula **1 – 3 – 5**

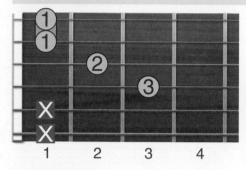

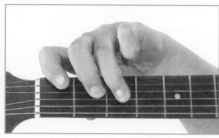

1   2   3   4

F

Alternate Names
F major, Fmaj, FM

Chord Notes   **F – A – C**
Chord Formula **1 – 3 – 5**

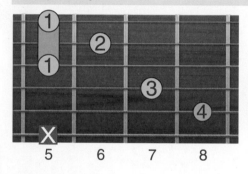

5   6   7   8

F

F

Alternate Names
F major, Fmaj, FM

Chord Notes   **F – A – C**
Chord Formula **1 – 3 – 5**

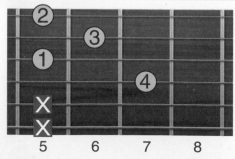

5   6   7   8

142

F7

Alternate Names
F seventh, Fdom7

Chord Notes   **F – A – C – E♭**
Chord Formula   **1 – 3 – 5 – ♭7**

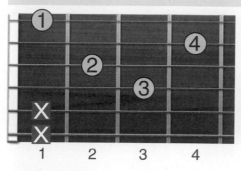

1   2   3   4

F7

Alternate Names
F seventh, Fdom7

Chord Notes   **F – A – C – E♭**
Chord Formula   **1 – 3 – 5 – ♭7**

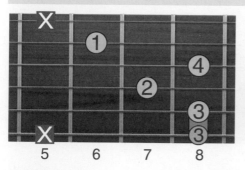

5   6   7   8

F7

Alternate Names
F seventh, Fdom7

Chord Notes   **F – A – C – E♭**
Chord Formula   **1 – 3 – 5 – ♭7**

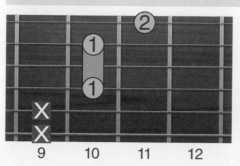

9   10   11   12

F

143

Fm

Alternate Names
F minor, Fmin, F–

Chord Notes **F – A♭ – C**
Chord Formula **1 – ♭3 – 5**

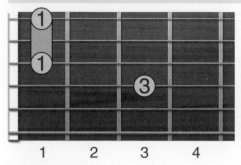

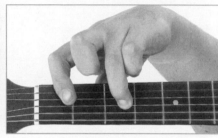

1   2   3   4

Fm

Alternate Names
F minor, Fmin, F–

Chord Notes **F – A♭ – C**
Chord Formula **1 – ♭3 – 5**

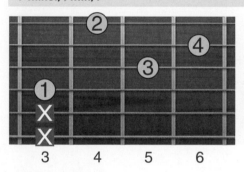

3   4   5   6

F

Fm

Alternate Names
F minor, Fmin, F–

Chord Notes **F – A♭ – C**
Chord Formula **1 – ♭3 – 5**

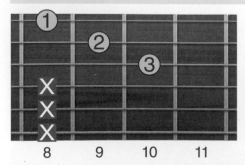

8   9   10   11

Fm7

Alternate Names
Fminor7, Fmin7, F–7

Chord Notes   **F – A♭ – C – E♭**
Chord Formula   **1 – ♭3 – 5 – ♭7**

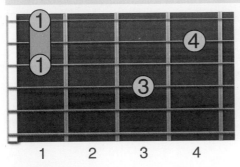

1   2   3   4

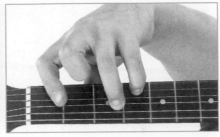

Fm7

Alternate Names
Fminor7, Fmin7, F–7

Chord Notes   **F – A♭ – C – E♭**
Chord Formula   **1 – ♭3 – 5 – ♭7**

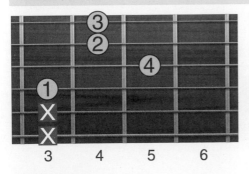

3   4   5   6

Fm7

Alternate Names
Fminor7, Fmin7, F–7

Chord Notes   **F – A♭ – C – E♭**
Chord Formula   **1 – ♭3 – 5 – ♭7**

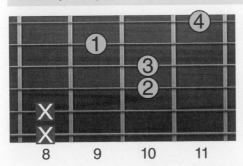

8   9   10   11

F

Fmaj7

Alternate Names
F Major7, FM7, FΔ7

Chord Notes   **F – A – C – E**
Chord Formula **1 – 3 – 5 – 7**

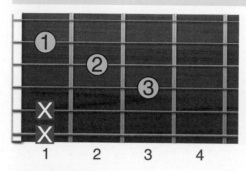

1   2   3   4

Fmaj7

Alternate Names
F Major7, FM7, FΔ7

Chord Notes   **F – A – C – E**
Chord Formula **1 – 3 – 5 – 7**

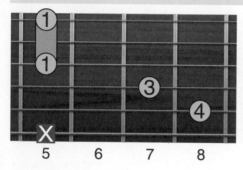

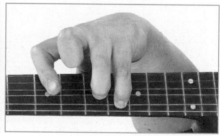

5   6   7   8

F

Fsus2

Alternate Names
F suspended second

Chord Notes   **F – G – C**
Chord Formula **1 – 2 – 5**

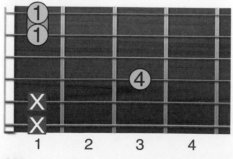

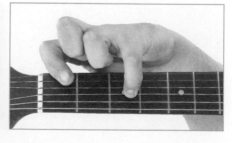

1   2   3   4

Fsus2

Alternate Names
F suspended second

Chord Notes   **F – G – C**
Chord Formula **1 – 2 – 5**

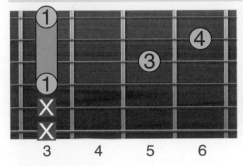

3   4   5   6

Fsus4

Alternate Names
F suspended fourth

Chord Notes   **F – B♭ – C**
Chord Formula **1 – 4 – 5**

1   2   3   4

Fsus4

Alternate Names
F suspended fourth

Chord Notes   **F – B♭ – C**
Chord Formula **1 – 4 – 5**

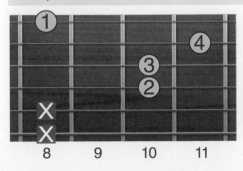

8   9   10   11

F

F7sus4

Alternate Names
F7 suspended fourth

Chord Notes   **F – B♭ – C – E♭**
Chord Formula   **1 – 4 – 5 – ♭7**

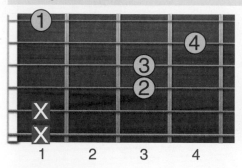

F7sus4

Alternate Names
F7 suspended fourth

Chord Notes   **F – B♭ – C – E♭**
Chord Formula   **1 – 4 – 5 – ♭7**

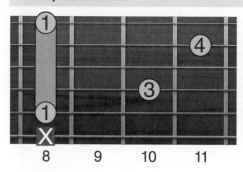
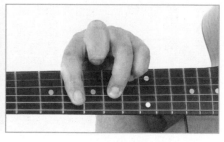

F

F6

Alternate Names
F sixth, F major 6, Fmaj6, FM6

Chord Notes   **F – A – C – D**
Chord Formula   **1 – 3 – 5 – 6**

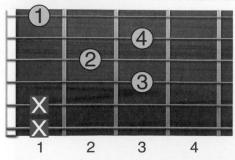

F6

Alternate Names
F sixth, F major 6, Fmaj6, FM6

Chord Notes **F – A – C – D**
Chord Formula **1 – 3 – 5 – 6**

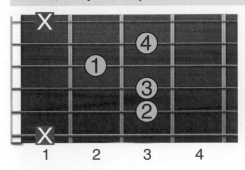

1 2 3 4

Fm6

Alternate Names
F minor sixth, Fmin6

Chord Notes **F – A♭ – C – D**
Chord Formula **1 – ♭3 – 5 – 6**

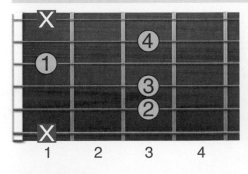

1 2 3 4

Fm6

Alternate Names
F minor sixth, Fmin6

Chord Notes **F – A♭ – C – D**
Chord Formula **1 – ♭3 – 5 – 6**

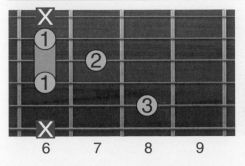

6 7 8 9

F

F9

Alternate Names
F ninth, Fdom9

Chord Notes   **F – A – C – E♭ – G**
Chord Formula   **1 – 3 – 5 – ♭7 – 9**

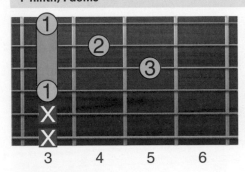

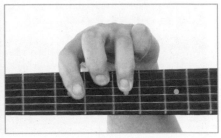

3   4   5   6

F9

Alternate Names
F ninth, Fdom9

Chord Notes   **F – A – C – E♭ – G**
Chord Formula   **1 – 3 – 5 – ♭7 – 9**

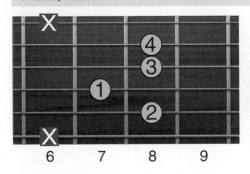

6   7   8   9

F

Fmaj9

Alternate Names
F major ninth, FM9, FΔ9

Chord Notes   **F – A – C – E – G**
Chord Formula   **1 – 3 – 5 – 7 – 9**

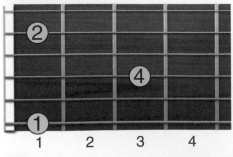

1   2   3   4

Fm9

Alternate Names
F minor ninth, Fmin9, F–9

Chord Notes   **F – A♭ – C – E♭ – G**
Chord Formula   **1 – ♭3 – 5 – ♭7 – 9**

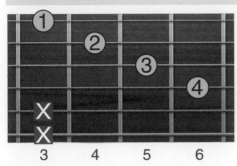

3   4   5   6

Fm9

Alternate Names
F minor ninth, Fmin9, F–9

Chord Notes   **F – A♭ – C – E♭ – G**
Chord Formula   **1 – ♭3 – 5 – ♭7 – 9**

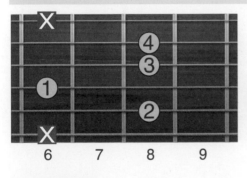

6   7   8   9

F6/9

Alternate Names
F six nine, F major sixth added 9

Chord Notes   **F – A – C – D – G**
Chord Formula   **1 – 3 – 5 – 6 – 9**

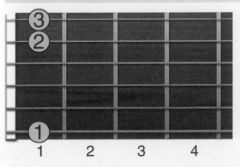

1   2   3   4

F

Faug

Alternate Names
F augmented, F+

Chord Notes   **F – A – C#**
Chord Formula   **1 – 3 – #5**

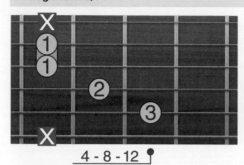

4 - 8 - 12

Faug

Alternate Names
F augmented, F+

Chord Notes   **F – A – C#**
Chord Formula   **1 – 3 – #5**

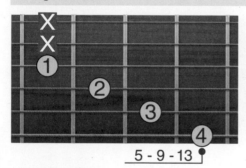

5 - 9 - 13

Fdim

Alternate Names
F diminished, F°

Chord Notes   **F – A♭ – B – D**
Chord Formula   **1 – ♭3 – ♭5 – ♭♭7**

1 - 4 - 7 - 10

F

152

Fdim

Alternate Names
F diminished, F°

Chord Notes **F – A♭ – B – D**
Chord Formula **1 – ♭3 – ♭5 – ♭♭7**

2 - 5 - 8 - 11

Fdim5

Alternate Names
F diminished fifth, F–5, F(♭5)

Chord Notes **F – A – B**
Chord Formula **1 – 3 – ♭5**

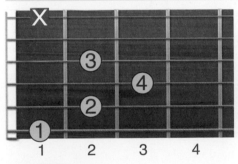

1   2   3   4

F

Fdim5

Alternate Names
F diminished fifth, F–5, F(♭5)

Chord Notes **F – A – B**
Chord Formula **1 – 3 – ♭5**

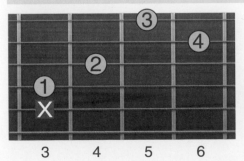

3   4   5   6

F7aug5

Chord Notes   **F – A – C# – E♭**
Chord Formula   **1 – 3 – #5 – ♭7**

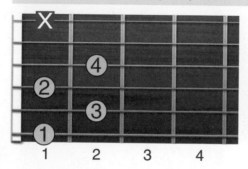

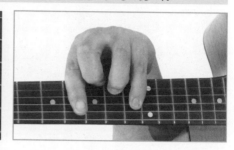

8   9   10   11

F7dim5

Chord Notes   **F – A – B – E♭**
Chord Formula   **1 – 3 – ♭5 – ♭7**

1   2   3   4

F

F7aug9

Chord Notes   **F – A – C – E♭ – G#**
Chord Formula   **1 – 3 – 5 – ♭7 – #9**

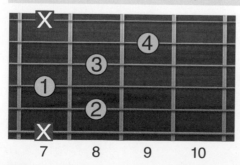

7   8   9   10

F7dim9

Alternate Names
F seventh diminished ninth, F7–9, F7♭9

Chord Notes   F – A – C – E♭ – G♭
Chord Formula   1 – 3 – 5 – ♭7 – ♭9

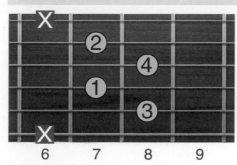

6   7   8   9

F11

Alternate Names
F eleventh

Chord Notes   F – A – C – E♭ – G – A
Chord Formula   1 – 3 – 5 – ♭7 – 9 – 11

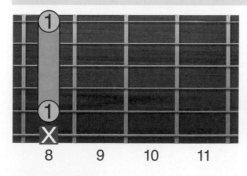

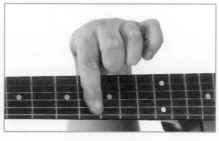

8   9   10   11

F

F13

Alternate Names
F thirteenth

Chord Notes   F – A – C – E♭ – G – D
Chord Formula   1 – 3 – 5 – ♭7 – 9 – 13

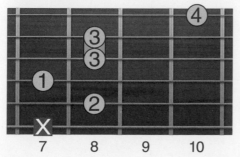

7   8   9   10

Music in the Key of F

Hey Jude – The Beatles

Smells Like Teen Spirit – Nirvana

Nothing Compares 2 U – Prince/Sinead O'Connor

The Wind Cries Mary – Jimi Hendrix

Brandenburg Concerto No. 1 and 2 in F major – Johann Sebastian Bach

F♯ G♭

The F♯ major scale consists of six sharps: F♯, G♯, A♯, C♯, D♯ and E♯ (for which you play an F). In this section of the chord dictionary, E♯ is represented as F for simplicity.

The F♯ minor scale consists of three sharps: F♯, G♯, C♯.

The G♭ major scale consists of six flats: G♭, A♭, B♭, C♭ (for which you play a B), D♭ and E♭. G♭ major is rarely used in music, as it has so many flattened notes that it is easier to refer to the F♯ major scale.

The G♭ minor scale is rarely used in music, as it has so many flattened notes that it is easier to refer to the F♯ minor scale.

This key has been featured in a number of powerful and grooving classic blues and rock songs, especially those that emphasise the minor aspect of the key. It is less common in orchestral music but can be found in a number of classical piano pieces.

The relative minor for F♯ major is D♯ minor.

The relative minor for G♭ major is E♭ minor.

F♯ Major Scale							
F♯	G♯	A♯	B	C♯	D♯	E♯ (F)	F♯
I	II	III	IV	V	VI	VII	I
1st	2nd	3rd	4th	5th	6th	7th	8th
	9th		11th		13th		

D♯ Minor Scale (Natural Minor)							
D♯	E♯ (F)	F♯	G♯	A♯	B	C♯	D♯
I	II	III	IV	V	VI	VII	I
1st	2nd	♭3rd	4th	5th	♭6th	♭7th	8th
	9th		11th		13th		

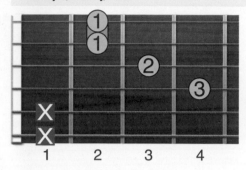

F#

Alternate Names
F# major, F#maj, F#M

Chord Notes **F# – A# – C#**
Chord Formula **1 – 3 – 5**

1   2   3   4

F#

Alternate Names
F# major, F#maj, F#M

Chord Notes **F# – A# – C#**
Chord Formula **1 – 3 – 5**

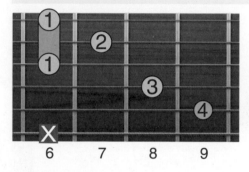

6   7   8   9

F#
G♭

F#

Alternate Names
F# major, F#maj, F#M

Chord Notes **F# – A# – C#**
Chord Formula **1 – 3 – 5**

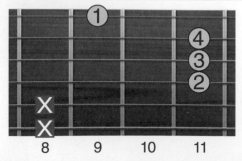

8   9   10   11

158

F#7

Alternate Names
F# seventh, F#dom7

Chord Notes   **F# – A# – C# – E**
Chord Formula   **1 – 3 – 5 – ♭7**

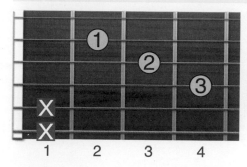

1   2   3   4

F#7

Alternate Names
F# seventh, F#dom7

Chord Notes   **F# – A# – C# – E**
Chord Formula   **1 – 3 – 5 – ♭7**

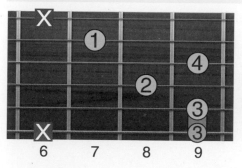

6   7   8   9

F#7

Alternate Names
F# seventh, F#dom7

Chord Notes   **F# – A# – C# – E**
Chord Formula   **1 – 3 – 5 – ♭7**

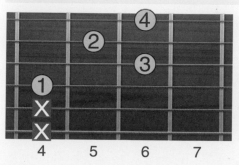

4   5   6   7

F#
G♭

F#m

Alternate Names
F# minor, F#min, F#–

Chord Notes   **F# – A – C#**
Chord Formula   **1 – ♭3 – 5**

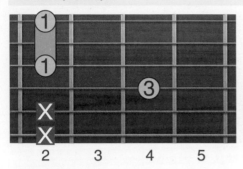

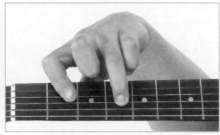

2   3   4   5

F#m

Alternate Names
F# minor, F#min, F#–

Chord Notes   **F# – A – C#**
Chord Formula   **1 – ♭3 – 5**

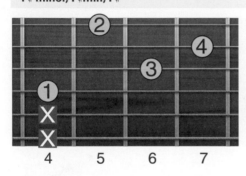

4   5   6   7

F#m

F#
G♭

Alternate Names
F# minor, F#min, F#–

Chord Notes   **F# – A – C#**
Chord Formula   **1 – ♭3 – 5**

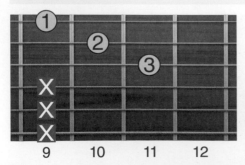

9   10   11   12

160

F#m7

Alternate Names
F#minor7, F#min7, F#–7

Chord Notes   **F# – A – C# – E**
Chord Formula   **1 – ♭3 – 5 – ♭7**

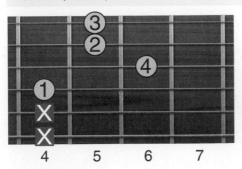

2   3   4   5

F#m7

Alternate Names
F#minor7, F#min7, F#–7

Chord Notes   **F# – A – C# – E**
Chord Formula   **1 – ♭3 – 5 – ♭7**

4   5   6   7

F#m7

Alternate Names
F#minor7, F#min7, F#–7

Chord Notes   **F# – A – C# – E**
Chord Formula   **1 – ♭3 – 5 – ♭7**

F#
G♭

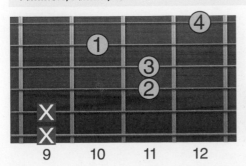

9   10   11   12

F#maj7

Alternate Names
F# Major7, F#M7, F#Δ7

Chord Notes **F# – A# – C# – F**
Chord Formula **1 – 3 – 5 – 7**

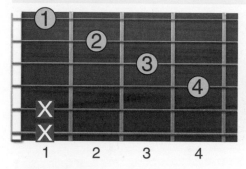
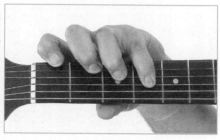

F#maj7

Alternate Names
F# Major7, F#M7, F#Δ7

Chord Notes **F# – A# – C# – F**
Chord Formula **1 – 3 – 5 – 7**

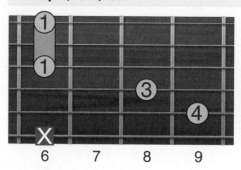
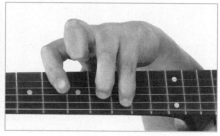

F#sus2

Alternate Names
F# suspended second

Chord Notes **F# – G# – C#**
Chord Formula **1 – 2 – 5**

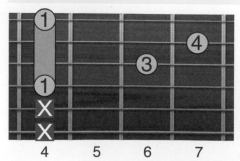
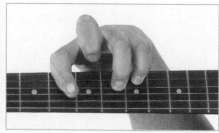

F#
G♭

F#sus2

Alternate Names	**Chord Notes** F# – G# – C#
F# suspended second	**Chord Formula** 1 – 2 – 5

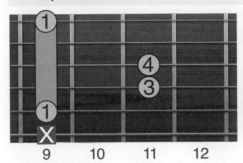
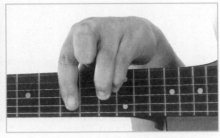

9   10   11   12

F#sus4

Alternate Names	**Chord Notes** F# – B – C#
F# suspended fourth	**Chord Formula** 1 – 4 – 5

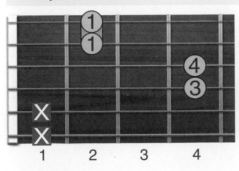

1   2   3   4

F#sus4

Alternate Names	**Chord Notes** F# – B – C#
F# suspended fourth	**Chord Formula** 1 – 4 – 5

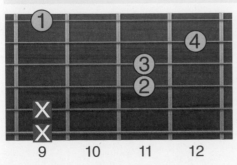

9   10   11   12

F#
G♭

F#7sus4

Alternate Names
F#7 suspended fourth

Chord Notes   **F# – B – C# – E**
Chord Formula   **1 – 4 – 5 – ♭7**

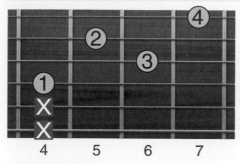

4   5   6   7

F#7sus4

Alternate Names
F#7 suspended fourth

Chord Notes   **F# – B – C# – E**
Chord Formula   **1 – 4 – 5 – ♭7**

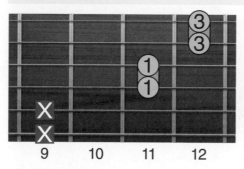

9   10   11   12

F#6

Alternate Names
F# sixth, F# major 6, F#maj6, F#M6

Chord Notes   **F# – A# – C# – D#**
Chord Formula   **1 – 3 – 5 – 6**

F#
G♭

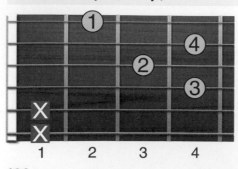

1   2   3   4

F#6

Alternate Names
F# sixth, F# major 6, F#maj6, F#M6

Chord Notes **F# – A# – C# – D#**
Chord Formula **1 – 3 – 5 – 6**

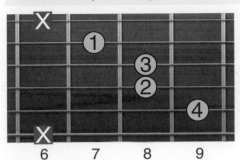

6   7   8   9

F#m6

Alternate Names
F# minor sixth, F#min6

Chord Notes **F# – A – C# – D#**
Chord Formula **1 – ♭3 – 5 – 6**

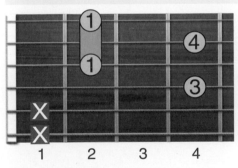

1   2   3   4

F#m6

Alternate Names
F# minor sixth, F#min6

Chord Notes **F# – A – C# – D#**
Chord Formula **1 – ♭3 – 5 – 6**

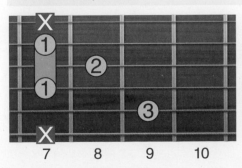

7   8   9   10

F#
G♭

165

F♯9

Alternate Names
F♯ ninth, F♯dom9

Chord Notes   **F♯ – A♯ – C♯ – E – G♯**
Chord Formula   **1 – 3 – 5 – ♭7 – 9**

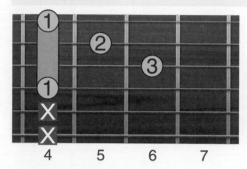

F♯9

Alternate Names
F♯ ninth, F♯dom9

Chord Notes   **F♯ – A♯ – C♯ – E – G♯**
Chord Formula   **1 – 3 – 5 – ♭7 – 9**

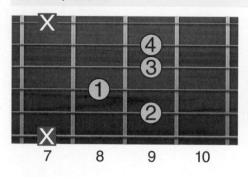

F♯maj9

F♯
G♭

Alternate Names
F♯ major ninth, F♯M9, F♯Δ9

Chord Notes   **F♯ – A♯ – C♯ – F – G♯**
Chord Formula   **1 – 3 – 5 – 7 – 9**

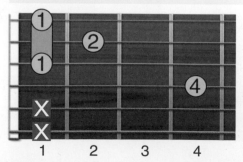

166

F#m9

Alternate Names
F# minor ninth, F#min9

Chord Notes **F# – A – C# – E – G#**
Chord Formula **1 – ♭3 – 5 – ♭7 – 9**

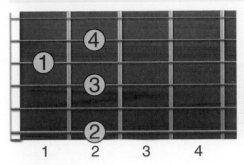

F#m9

Alternate Names
F# minor ninth, F#min9

Chord Notes **F# – A – C# – E – G#**
Chord Formula **1 – ♭3 – 5 – ♭7 – 9**

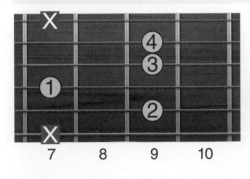

F#6/9

Alternate Names
F# six nine, F# major sixth added 9

Chord Notes **F# – A# – C# – D# – G#**
Chord Formula **1 – 3 – 5 – 6 – 9**

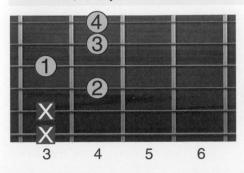

F#
G♭

F#aug

Alternate Names
F# augmented, F#+

Chord Notes   **F# – A# – D**
Chord Formula   **1 – 3 – #5**

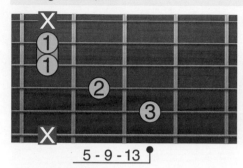

5 - 9 - 13

F#aug

Alternate Names
F# augmented, F#+

Chord Notes   **F# – A# – D**
Chord Formula   **1 – 3 – #5**

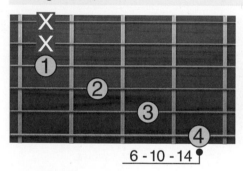

6 - 10 - 14

F#dim

Alternate Names
F# diminished, F#°

Chord Notes   **F# – A – C – E♭**
Chord Formula   **1 – ♭3 – ♭5 – ♭♭7**

F#
G♭

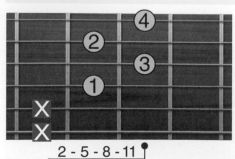

2 - 5 - 8 - 11

168

F#dim

Alternate Names
F# diminished, F#°

Chord Notes   **F# – A – C – E♭**
Chord Formula   **1 – ♭3 – ♭5 – ♭♭7**

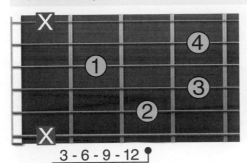
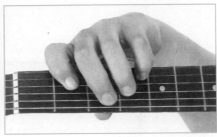

3 - 6 - 9 - 12

F#dim5

Alternate Names
F# diminished fifth, F#–5, F#(♭5)

Chord Notes   **F# – A# – C**
Chord Formula   **1 – 3 – ♭5**

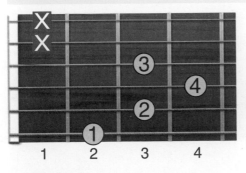

1   2   3   4

F#dim5

Alternate Names
F# diminished fifth, F#–5, C#(♭5)

Chord Notes   **F# – A# – C**
Chord Formula   **1 – 3 – ♭5**

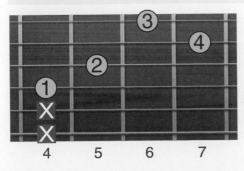

4   5   6   7

F#
G♭

F#7aug5

Alternate Names
F# seventh augmented fifth, F#7+5, F#7#5

Chord Notes **F# – A# – D – E**
Chord Formula **1 – 3 – #5 – b7**

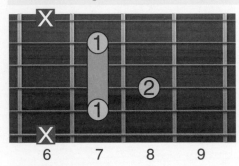

6   7   8   9

F#7dim5

Alternate Names
F# seventh diminished fifth, F#7–5, F#7b5

Chord Notes **F# – A# – C – E**
Chord Formula **1 – 3 – b5 – b7**

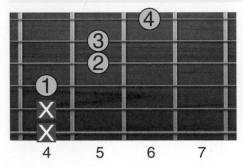

4   5   6   7

F#7aug9

F#
Gb

Alternate Names
F# seventh augmented ninth, F#7+9, F#7#9

Chord Notes **F# – A# – C# – E – A**
Chord Formula **1 – 3 – 5 – b7 – #9**

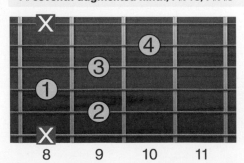

8   9   10   11

F#7dim9

Alternate Names
F# seventh diminished ninth, F#7–9, F#7♭9

Chord Notes   F# – A# – C# – E – G
Chord Formula   1 – 3 – 5 – ♭7 – ♭9

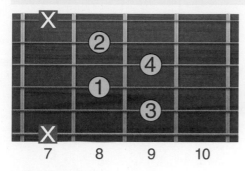

F#11

Alternate Names
F# eleventh

Chord Notes   F# – A# – C# – E – G# – B
Chord Formula   1 – 3 – 5 – ♭7 – 9 – 11

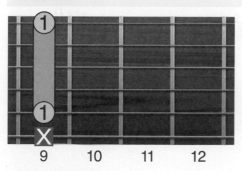

F#13

Alternate Names
F# thirteenth

Chord Notes   F# – A# – C# – E – G# – D#
Chord Formula   1 – 3 – 5 – ♭7 – 9 – 13

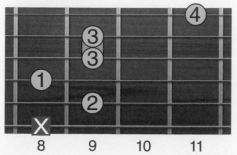

F#
G♭

Music in the Key of F♯/G♭

Immigrant Song – Led Zeppelin

Foxy Lady – Jimi Hendrix

Wonderwall – Oasis

Billie Jean – Michael Jackson

Yellow Submarine – The Beatles (the guitars are actually tuned down a semitone, thus sound lower: i.e. the G chord shapes sound as G♭ chords)

Piano Sonata, Op. 78 – Ludwig van Beethoven

G

The G major scale consists of one sharp: F#.

The G minor scale consists of two flats: B♭ and G♭.

The key of G is a popular key for country, folk and bluegrass styles. It complements other instruments such as mandolin, fiddle and the banjo, which is tuned to open G. It is generally a bright and happy key. G minor on the other hand can be mournful yet powerful.

The relative minor for G major is E minor.

G Major Scale							
G	A	B	C	D	E	F#	G
I	II	III	IV	V	VI	VII	I
1st	2nd	3rd	4th	5th	6th	7th	8th
	9th		11th		13th		

E Minor Scale (Natural Minor)							
E	F#	G	A	B	C	D	E
I	II	III	IV	V	VI	VII	I
1st	2nd	♭3rd	4th	5th	♭6th	♭7th	8th
	9th		11th		13th		

G

Alternate Names
G major, Gmaj, GM

Chord Notes   **G – B – D**
Chord Formula   **1 – 3 – 5**

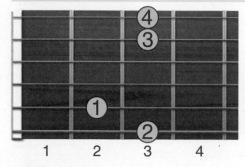

1   2   3   4

G

Alternate Names
G major, Gmaj, GM

Chord Notes   **G – B – D**
Chord Formula   **1 – 3 – 5**

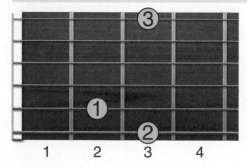

1   2   3   4

G

Alternate Names
G major, Gmaj, GM

Chord Notes   **G – B – D**
Chord Formula   **1 – 3 – 5**

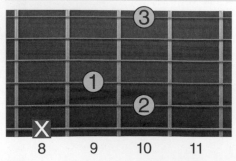

8   9   10   11

G

G7

Alternate Names
G seventh, Gdom7

Chord Notes   **G – B – D – F**
Chord Formula **1 – 3 – 5 – ♭7**

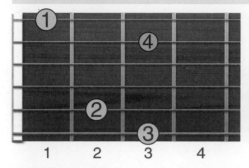 

1   2   3   4

G7

Alternate Names
G seventh, Gdom7

Chord Notes   **G – B – D – F**
Chord Formula **1 – 3 – 5 – ♭7**

1   2   3   4

G7

Alternate Names
G seventh, Gdom7

Chord Notes   **G – B – D – F**
Chord Formula **1 – 3 – 5 – ♭7**

7   8   9   10

G

Gm

Chord Notes **G – B♭ – D**
Chord Formula **1 – ♭3 – 5**

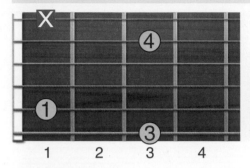
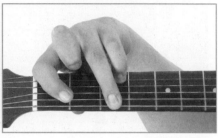

| 1 | 2 | 3 | 4 |

Gm

Alternate Names
G minor, Gmin, G–

Chord Notes **G – B♭ – D**
Chord Formula **1 – ♭3 – 5**

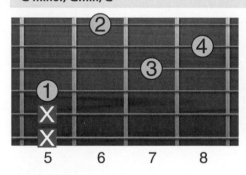

| 5 | 6 | 7 | 8 |

Gm

Alternate Names
G minor, Gmin, G–

Chord Notes **G – B♭ – D**
Chord Formula **1 – ♭3 – 5**

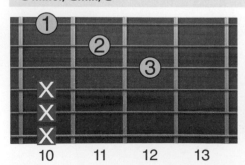

| 10 | 11 | 12 | 13 |

G

Gm7

Alternate Names
Gminor7, Gmin7, G–7

Chord Notes   **G – B♭ – D – F**
Chord Formula   **1 – ♭3 – 5 – ♭7**

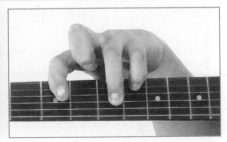

     3   4   5   6

Gm7

Alternate Names
Gminor7, Gmin7, G–7

Chord Notes   **G – B♭ – D – F**
Chord Formula   **1 – ♭3 – 5 – ♭7**

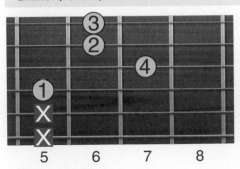

     5   6   7   8

Gm7

Alternate Names
Gminor7, Gmin7, G–7

Chord Notes   **G – B♭ – D – F**
Chord Formula   **1 – ♭3 – 5 – ♭7**

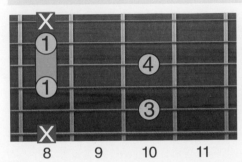

     8   9   10   11

G

Gmaj7

Alternate Names
G Major7, GM7, GΔ7

Chord Notes   **G – B – D – F♯**
Chord Formula **1 – 3 – 5 – 7**

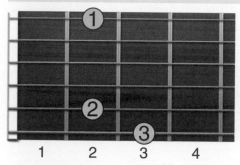

1   2   3   4

Gmaj7

Alternate Names
G Major7, GM7, GΔ7

Chord Notes   **G – B – D – F♯**
Chord Formula **1 – 3 – 5 – 7**

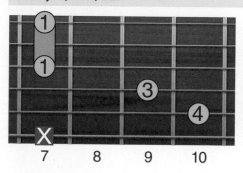
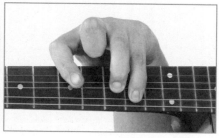

7   8   9   10

Gsus2

Alternate Names
G suspended second

Chord Notes   **G – A – D**
Chord Formula **1 – 2 – 5**

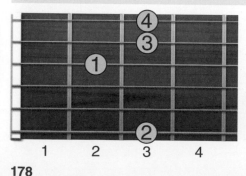

1   2   3   4

G

178

Gsus2

Alternate Names	Chord Notes	G – A – D
G suspended second	Chord Formula	**1 – 2 – 5**

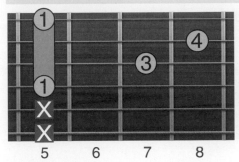 

5   6   7   8

Gsus4

Alternate Names	Chord Notes	G – C – D
G suspended fourth	Chord Formula	**1 – 4 – 5**

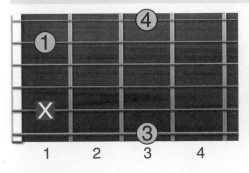 

1   2   3   4

Gsus4

Alternate Names	Chord Notes	G – C – D
G suspended fourth	Chord Formula	**1 – 4 – 5**

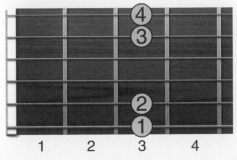 

1   2   3   4

G

G7sus4

Alternate Names
G7 suspended fourth

Chord Notes   **G – C – D – F**
Chord Formula   **1 – 4 – 5 – ♭7**

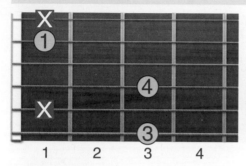

G7sus4

Alternate Names
G7 suspended fourth

Chord Notes   **G – C – D – F**
Chord Formula   **1 – 4 – 5 – ♭7**

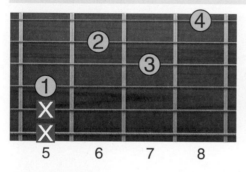

G6

Alternate Names
G sixth, G major 6, Gmaj6, GM6

Chord Notes   **G – B – D – E**
Chord Formula   **1 – 3 – 5 – 6**

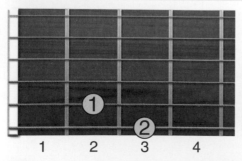

G

180

G6

Alternate Names
G sixth, G major 6, Gmaj6, GM6

Chord Notes   **G – B – D – E**
Chord Formula   **1 – 3 – 5 – 6**

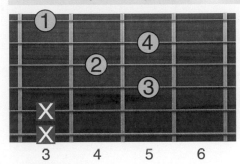
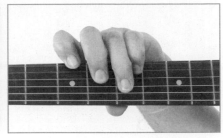

3   4   5   6

Gm6

Alternate Names
G minor sixth, Gmin6

Chord Notes   **G – B♭ – D – E**
Chord Formula   **1 – ♭3 – 5 – 6**

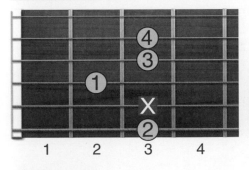

1   2   3   4

Gm6

Alternate Names
G minor sixth, Gmin6

Chord Notes   **G – B♭ – D – E**
Chord Formula   **1 – ♭3 – 5 – 6**

8   9   10   11

G

G9

Alternate Names
G ninth, Gdom9

Chord Notes   **G – B – D – F – A**
Chord Formula   **1 – 3 – 5 – ♭7 – 9**

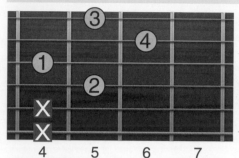

G9

Alternate Names
G ninth, Gdom9

Chord Notes   **G – B – D – F – A**
Chord Formula   **1 – 3 – 5 – ♭7 – 9**

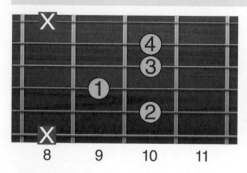

Gmaj9

Alternate Names
G major ninth, GM9, G∆9

Chord Notes   **G – B – D – F♯ – A**
Chord Formula   **1 – 3 – 5 – 7 – 9**

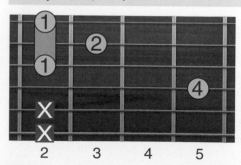
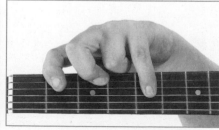

G

182

Gm9

Alternate Names
G minor ninth, Gmin9, G–9

Chord Notes   **G – Bb – D – F – A**
Chord Formula   **1 – b3 – 5 – b7 – 9**

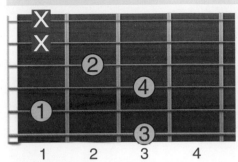

1   2   3   4

Gm9

Alternate Names
G minor ninth, Gmin9, G–9

Chord Notes   **G – Bb – D – F – A**
Chord Formula   **1 – b3 – 5 – b7 – 9**

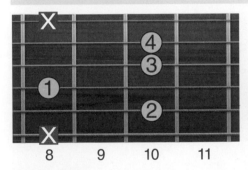

8   9   10   11

G6/9

Alternate Names
G six nine, G major sixth added 9

Chord Notes   **G – B – D – E – A**
Chord Formula   **1 – 3 – 5 – 6 – 9**

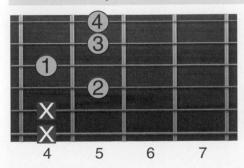

4   5   6   7

G

183

Gaug

Alternate Names
G augmented, G+

Chord Notes **G – B – D#**
Chord Formula **1 – 3 – #5**

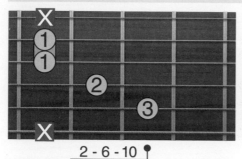

2 - 6 - 10

Gaug

Alternate Names
G augmented, G+

Chord Notes **G – B – D#**
Chord Formula **1 – 3 – #5**

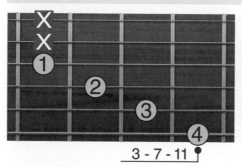

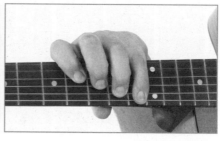

3 - 7 - 11

Gdim

Alternate Names
G diminished, G°

Chord Notes **G – B♭ – D♭ – E**
Chord Formula **1 – ♭3 – ♭5 – ♭♭7**

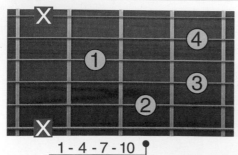

1 - 4 - 7 - 10

G

Gdim

Alternate Names
G diminished, G°

Chord Notes **G – B♭ – D♭ – E**
Chord Formula **1 – ♭3 – ♭5 – ♭♭7**

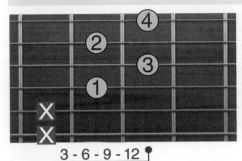

3 - 6 - 9 - 12

Gdim5

Alternate Names
G diminished fifth, G–5, G(♭5)

Chord Notes **G – B – D♭**
Chord Formula **1 – 3 – ♭5**

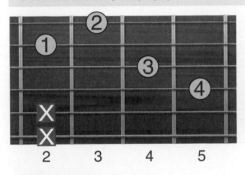

2   3   4   5

Gdim5

Alternate Names
G diminished fifth, G–5, G(♭5)

Chord Notes **G – B – D♭**
Chord Formula **1 – 3 – ♭5**

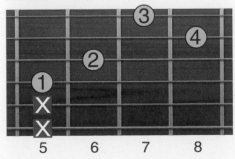

5   6   7   8

G

G7aug5

Alternate Names
G seventh augmented fifth, G7+5, G7#5

Chord Notes **G – B – D# – F**
Chord Formula **1 – 3 – #5 – ♭7**

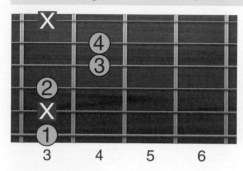

G7dim5

Alternate Names
G seventh diminished fifth, G7–5, G7♭5

Chord Notes **G – B – D♭ – F**
Chord Formula **1 – 3 – ♭5 – ♭7**

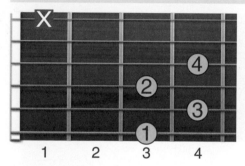

G7aug9

Alternate Names
G seventh augmented ninth, G7+9, G7#9

Chord Notes **G – B – D – F – A#**
Chord Formula **1 – 3 – 5 – ♭7 – #9**

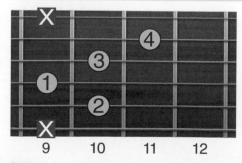

G

G7dim9

Alternate Names
G seventh diminished ninth, G7–9, G7♭9

Chord Notes   **G – B – D – F – A♭**
Chord Formula   **1 – 3 – 5 – ♭7 – ♭9**

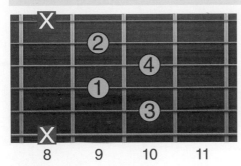

| 8 | 9 | 10 | 11 |

G11

Alternate Names
G eleventh

Chord Notes   **G – B – D – F – A – C**
Chord Formula   **1 – 3 – 5 – ♭7 – 9 – 11**

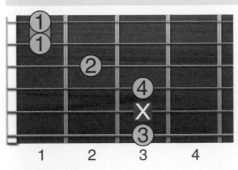

| 1 | 2 | 3 | 4 |

G13

Alternate Names
G thirteenth

Chord Notes   **G – B – D – F – A – E**
Chord Formula   **1 – 3 – 5 – ♭7 – 9 – 13**

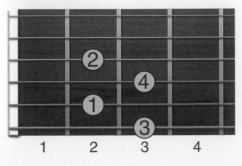

| 1 | 2 | 3 | 4 |

G

187

Music in the Key of G

Knockin' on Heaven's Door – Bob Dylan

Brown Eyed Girl – Van Morrison

Blackbird – The Beatles

Wish You Were Here – Pink Floyd

Blister in the Sun – Violent Femmes

Serenade No. 13 for strings in G major (Eine kleine Nachtmusik) – Wolfgang Amadeus Mozart

The A♭ major scale consists of four flats: A♭, B♭, D♭ and E♭.

The A♭ minor scale consists of seven flats: A♭, B♭, C♭ (for which you play a B), D♭, E♭, F♭ (for which you play an E) and G♭.

The G♯ major scale consists of six sharps and one double sharp: G♯, A♯, B♯ (for which you play a C), C♯,D♯, E♯ (for which you play an F) and F♯♯ (for which you play a G). G♯ major is rarely used in music, as it has so many sharpened notes that it is easier to refer to the A♭ major scale.

The G♯ minor scale consists of five sharps: G♯, A♯, C♯, D♯ and F♯.

G♯ is not a common key for the guitar and generally isn't utilised much unless it is played using open chords with a capo. It is used in keyboard music, providing significant challenges to pianists for centuries. The A♭ key is generally preferred by horn players, especially jazz musicians.

The relative minor for G♯ major is E♯ minor.

The relative minor for A♭ major is F minor.

A♭ Major Scale							
A♭	B♭	C	D♭	E♭	F	G	A♭
I	II	III	IV	V	VI	VII	I
1st	2nd	3rd	4th	5th	6th	7th	8th
	9th		11th		13th		

F Minor Scale (Natural Minor)							
F	G	A♭	B♭	C	D♭	E♭	F
I	II	III	IV	V	VI	VII	I
1st	2nd	♭3rd	4th	5th	♭6th	♭7th	8th
	9th		11th		13th		

A♭

Alternate Names
A♭ major, A♭maj, A♭M

Chord Notes   **A♭ – C – E♭**
Chord Formula   **1 – 3 – 5**

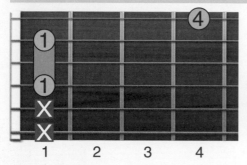

1   2   3   4

A♭

Alternate Names
A♭ major, A♭maj, A♭M

Chord Notes   **A♭ – C – E♭**
Chord Formula   **1 – 3 – 5**

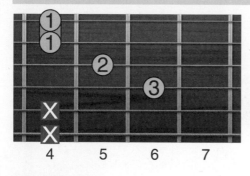

4   5   6   7

A♭

Alternate Names
A♭ major, A♭maj, A♭M

Chord Notes   **A♭ – C – E♭**
Chord Formula   **1 – 3 – 5**

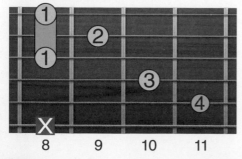

8   9   10   11

G♯
A♭

A♭7

Chord Notes   **A♭ – C – E♭ – G♭**
Chord Formula   **1 – 3 – 5 – ♭7**

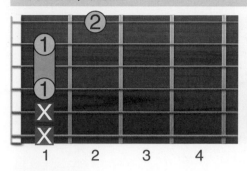

1   2   3   4

A♭7

Chord Notes   **A♭ – C – E♭ – G♭**
Chord Formula   **1 – 3 – 5 – ♭7**

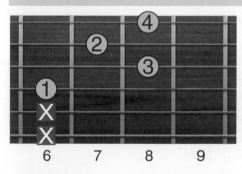

6   7   8   9

A♭7

Chord Notes   **A♭ – C – E♭ – G♭**
Chord Formula   **1 – 3 – 5 – ♭7**

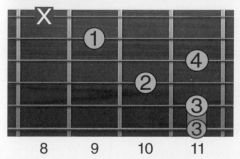

8   9   10   11

G♯
A♭

A♭m

Alternate Names
A♭ minor, A♭min, A♭–

Chord Notes   **A♭ – B – E♭**
Chord Formula   **1 – ♭3 – 5**

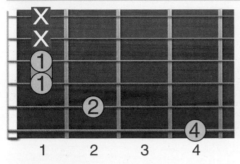
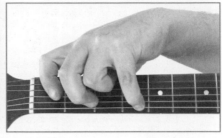

A♭m

Alternate Names
A♭ minor, A♭min, A♭–

Chord Notes   **A♭ – B – E♭**
Chord Formula   **1 – ♭3 – 5**

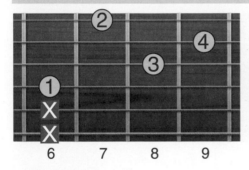
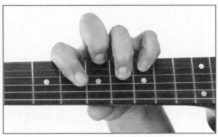

A♭m

Alternate Names
A♭ minor, A♭min, A♭–

Chord Notes   **A♭ – B – E♭**
Chord Formula   **1 – ♭3 – 5**

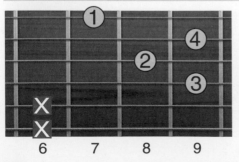

G#
A♭

Abm7

Alternate Names
Abminor7, Abmin7, Ab–7

Chord Notes   Ab – B – Eb – Gb
Chord Formula   1 – b3 – 5 – b7

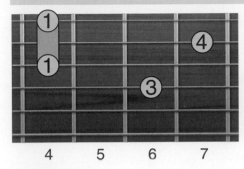

4   5   6   7

Abm7

Alternate Names
Abminor7, Abmin7, Ab–7

Chord Notes   Ab – B – Eb – Gb
Chord Formula   1 – b3 – 5 – b7

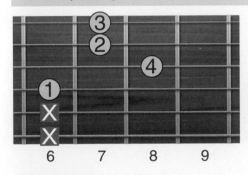

6   7   8   9

Abm7

Alternate Names
Abminor7, Abmin7, Ab–7

Chord Notes   Ab – B – Eb – Gb
Chord Formula   1 – b3 – 5 – b7

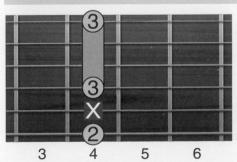
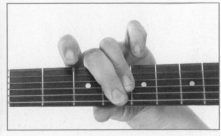

3   4   5   6

G#
Ab

A♭maj7

Alternate Names
A♭ Major7, A♭M7, A♭Δ7

Chord Notes   **A♭ – C – E♭ – G**
Chord Formula   **1 – 3 – 5 – 7**

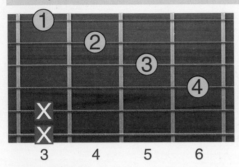

3   4   5   6

A♭maj7

Alternate Names
A♭ Major7, A♭M7, A♭Δ7

Chord Notes   **A♭ – C – E♭ – G**
Chord Formula   **1 – 3 – 5 – 7**

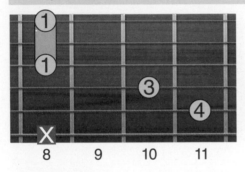

8   9   10   11

A♭sus2

Alternate Names
A♭ suspended second

Chord Notes   **A♭ – B♭ – E♭**
Chord Formula   **1 – 2 – 5**

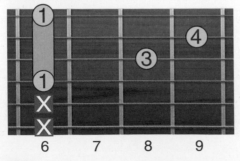
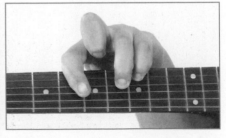

6   7   8   9

G♯
A♭

194

A♭sus2

Alternate Names
A♭ suspended second

Chord Notes   **A♭ – B♭ – E♭**
Chord Formula   **1 – 2 – 5**

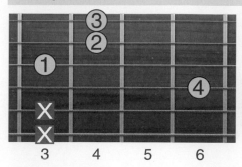

A♭sus4

Alternate Names
A♭ suspended fourth

Chord Notes   **A♭ – D♭ – E♭**
Chord Formula   **1 – 4 – 5**

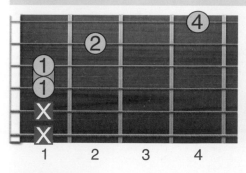

A♭sus4

Alternate Names
A♭ suspended fourth

Chord Notes   **A♭ – D♭ – E♭**
Chord Formula   **1 – 4 – 5**

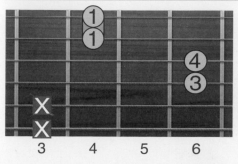

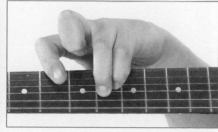

G#
A♭

A♭7sus4

Alternate Names
A♭7 suspended fourth

Chord Notes **A♭ – D♭ – E♭ – G♭**
Chord Formula **1 – 4 – 5 – ♭7**

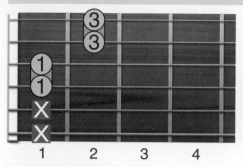

1 2 3 4

A♭7sus4

Alternate Names
A♭7 suspended fourth

Chord Notes **A♭ – D♭ – E♭ – G♭**
Chord Formula **1 – 4 – 5 – ♭7**

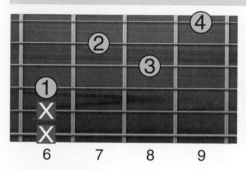

6 7 8 9

A♭6

Alternate Names
A♭ sixth, A♭ major 6, A♭maj6, A♭M6

Chord Notes **A♭ – C – E♭ – F**
Chord Formula **1 – 3 – 5 – 6**

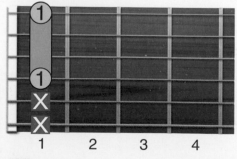

1 2 3 4

G♯
A♭

196

A♭6

Alternate Names
A♭ sixth, A♭ major 6, A♭maj6, A♭M6

Chord Notes   A♭ – C – E♭ – F
Chord Formula   1 – 3 – 5 – 6

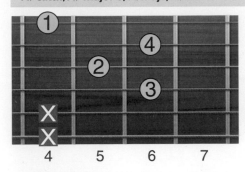

4   5   6   7

A♭m6

Alternate Names
A♭ minor sixth, A♭min6

Chord Notes   A♭ – B – E♭ – F
Chord Formula   1 – ♭3 – 5 – 6

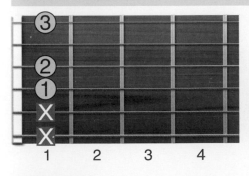

1   2   3   4

A♭m6

Alternate Names
A♭ minor sixth, A♭min6

Chord Notes   A♭ – B – E♭ – F
Chord Formula   1 – ♭3 – 5 – 6

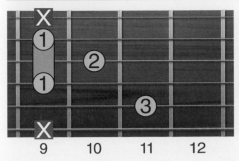

9   10   11   12

G#
A♭

197

A♭9

Alternate Names
A♭ ninth, A♭dom9

Chord Notes   **A♭ – C – E♭ – G♭ – B♭**
Chord Formula   **1 – 3 – 5 – ♭7 – 9**

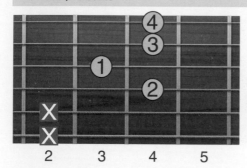

| 2 | 3 | 4 | 5 |

A♭9

Alternate Names
A♭ ninth, A♭dom9

Chord Notes   **A♭ – C – E♭ – G♭ – B♭**
Chord Formula   **1 – 3 – 5 – ♭7 – 9**

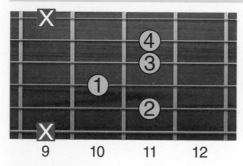

| 9 | 10 | 11 | 12 |

A♭maj9

Alternate Names
A♭ major ninth, A♭M9, A♭Δ9

Chord Notes   **A♭ – C – E♭ – G – B♭**
Chord Formula   **1 – 3 – 5 – 7 – 9**

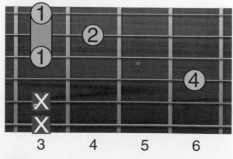
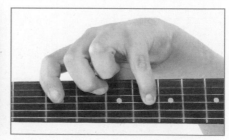

| 3 | 4 | 5 | 6 |

G#
A♭

A♭m9

Alternate Names
A♭ minor ninth, A♭min9, A♭–9

Chord Notes   A♭ – B – E♭ – G♭ – B♭
Chord Formula   1 – ♭3 – 5 – ♭7 – 9

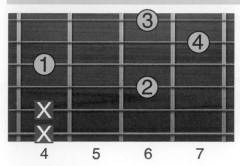
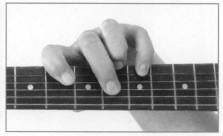

4   5   6   7

A♭m9

Alternate Names
A♭ minor ninth, A♭min9, A♭–9

Chord Notes   A♭ – B – E♭ – G♭ – B♭
Chord Formula   1 – ♭3 – 5 – ♭7 – 9

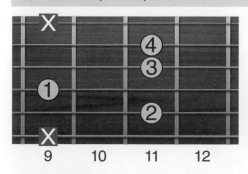

9   10   11   12

A♭6/9

Alternate Names
A♭ six nine, A♭ major sixth added 9

Chord Notes   A♭ – C – E♭ – F – B♭
Chord Formula   1 – 3 – 5 – 6 – 9

5   6   7   8

G#
A♭

A♭aug

Alternate Names
A♭ augmented, A♭+

Chord Notes   **A♭ – C – E**
Chord Formula   **1 – 3 – ♯5**

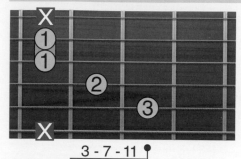

3 - 7 - 11

A♭aug

Alternate Names
A♭ augmented, A♭+

Chord Notes   **A♭ – C – E**
Chord Formula   **1 – 3 – ♯5**

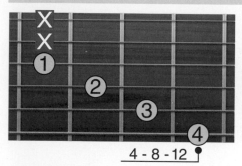

4 - 8 - 12

A♭dim

Alternate Names
A♭ diminished, A♭°

Chord Notes   **A♭ – B – D – F**
Chord Formula   **1 – ♭3 – ♭5 – ♭♭7**

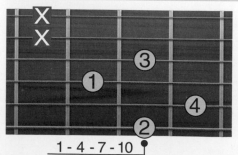

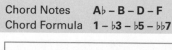

1 - 4 - 7 - 10

G♯
A♭

A♭dim

Alternate Names
A♭ diminished, A♭°

Chord Notes **A♭ – B – D – F**
Chord Formula **1 – ♭3 – ♭5 – ♭♭7**

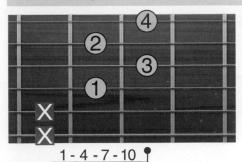

1 - 4 - 7 - 10

A♭dim5

Alternate Names
A♭ diminished fifth, A♭–5, A♭(♭5)

Chord Notes **A♭ – C – D**
Chord Formula **1 – 3 – ♭5**

3   4   5   6

A♭dim5

Alternate Names
A♭ diminished fifth, A♭–5, A♭(♭5)

Chord Notes **A♭ – C – D**
Chord Formula **1 – 3 – ♭5**

4   5   6   7

G#
A♭

A♭7aug5

Alternate Names
A♭ seventh augmented fifth, A♭7+5, A♭7#5

Chord Notes   **A♭ – C – E – G♭**
Chord Formula   **1 – 3 – #5 – ♭7**

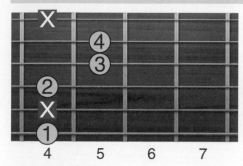

A♭7dim5

Alternate Names
A♭ seventh diminished fifth, A♭7–5, A♭7♭5

Chord Notes   **A♭ – C – D – G♭**
Chord Formula   **1 – 3 – ♭5 – ♭7**

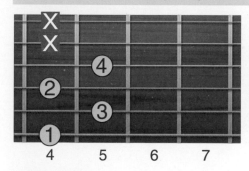

A♭7aug9

Alternate Names
A♭ seventh augmented ninth, A♭7+9, A♭7#9

Chord Notes   **A♭ – C – E♭ – G♭ – B**
Chord Formula   **1 – 3 – 5 – ♭7 – #9**

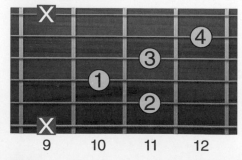

G#
A♭

A♭7dim9

Alternate Names
A♭ seventh diminished ninth, A♭7–9, A♭7♭9

Chord Notes   A♭ – C – E♭ – G♭ – A
Chord Formula   1 – 3 – 5 – ♭7 – ♭9

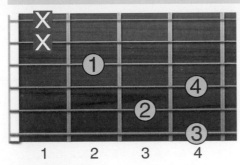

1   2   3   4

A♭11

Alternate Names
A♭ eleventh

Chord Notes   A♭ – C – E♭ – G♭ – B♭ – D♭
Chord Formula   1 – 3 – 5 – ♭7 – 9 – 11

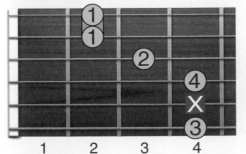

1   2   3   4

A♭13

Alternate Names
A♭ thirteenth

Chord Notes   A♭ – C – E♭ – G♭ – B♭ – F
Chord Formula   1 – 3 – 5 – ♭7 – 9 – 13

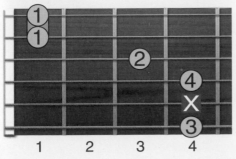

1   2   3   4

G♯
A♭

203

Music in the Key of G♯/A♭

Buddy Holly – Weezer

Piggies – The Beatles

Easy – Commodores/Faith No More

Walkin' on the Sun – Smash Mouth

Symphony No. 1 in A-flat major – Edward Elgar

Moveable Chords

This section covers most moveable chords you are likely to need. Moveable chords include barre chords and power chords, as well as other shapes that can be played anywhere on the fretboard.

There are usually three or four places up the neck to play the same chord. This is very helpful when playing chord progressions because you don't want to make too much work for yourself when changing chords.

For example, if you have a progression that goes from E7aug9 (page 138) to the first A major chord (page 14), you will have to move right down the guitar and up again for every change.

A much more economical way to play this is to go from the E7aug9 to an A major barre chord (the first barre chord on page 212 played on the fifth fret). In essence, a little more practice on these chords will make playing chord progressions a lot easier in the long run.

Power chords are almost essential in rock music. A power chord is also known as a one/five chord because you only play the **first** and the **fifth** notes. This means that the chord is neither a major nor a minor, and will therefore fit in whether the rest of the band is playing in the major or minor key.

Power chords sound particularly good on an electric guitar with distortion and – because they don't include the third note – sound clean and even. Because of the simplicity of the power chord patterns, it is possible to change chords at lightning speed and therefore they are a favourite of heavy metal players.

Here are the open power chords in two and three note versions.

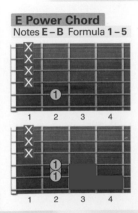

E Power Chord
Notes E – B Formula 1 – 5

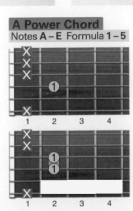

A Power Chord
Notes A – E Formula 1 – 5

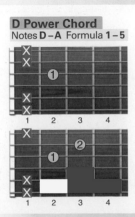

D Power Chord
Notes D – A Formula 1 – 5

The diagrams in this section show the root note for the chord in orange. Use this fretboard diagram to ascertain which key to play the chord in. For example, in the first chord diagram (Major: D formation), the root note is played on the B string with the third finger.

	1	2	3	4	5	6	7	8	9	10	11	12	
E	F	F#/Gb	G	G#/Ab	A	A#/Bb	B	C	C#/Db	D	D#/Eb	E	E
B	C	C#/Db	D	D#/Eb	E	F	F#/Gb	G	G#/Ab	A	A#/Bb	B	B
G	G#/Ab	A	A#/Bb	B	C	C#/Db	D	D#/Eb	E	F	F#/Gb	G	G
D	D#/Eb	E	F	F#/Gb	G	G#/Ab	A	A#/Bb	B	C	C#/Db	D	D
A	A#/Bb	B	C	C#/Db	D	D#/Eb	E	F	F#/Gb	G	G#/Ab	A	A
E	F	F#/Gb	G	G#/Ab	A	A#/Bb	B	C	C#/Db	D	D#/Eb	E	E
Fret	1	2	3	4	5	6	7	8	9	10	11	12	

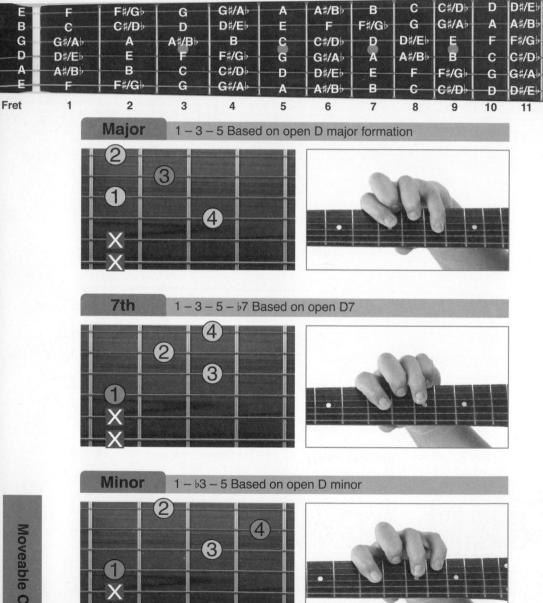

Major   1 – 3 – 5 Based on open D major formation

7th   1 – 3 – 5 – ♭7 Based on open D7

Minor   1 – ♭3 – 5 Based on open D minor

Min 7th 1 – ♭3 – 5 – ♭7 Based on open D minor 7

Major 1 – 3 – 5 Based on open A major

7th 1 – 3 – 5 – ♭7 Based on open A7

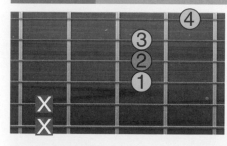 

Minor 1 – ♭3 – 5 Based on open A minor

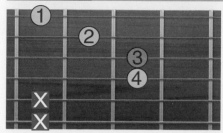 

Moveable Chords

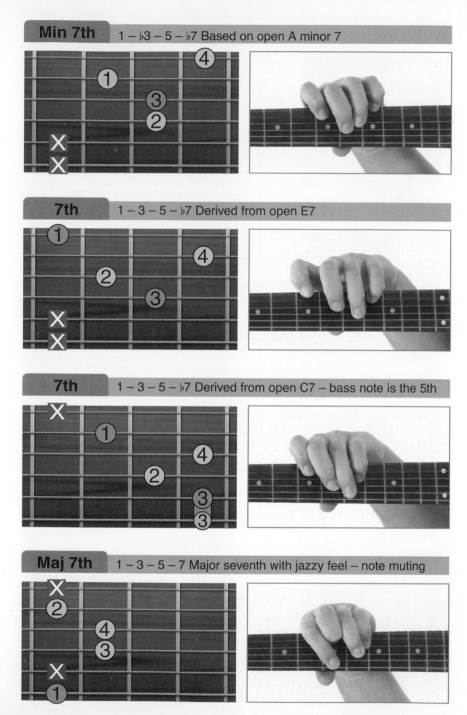

Min 7th   1 – ♭3 – 5 – ♭7 Based on open A minor 7

7th   1 – 3 – 5 – ♭7 Derived from open E7

7th   1 – 3 – 5 – ♭7 Derived from open C7 – bass note is the 5th

Maj 7th   1 – 3 – 5 – 7 Major seventh with jazzy feel – note muting

6th 1 – 3 – 5 – 6 Based on open F6

6th 1 – 3 – 5 – 6 Based on open E major 6

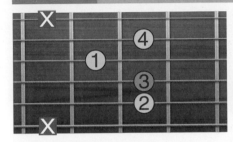

Min 6th 1 – ♭3 – 5 – 6 Based on open A minor 6

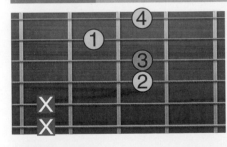

Min 6th 1 – ♭3 – 5 – 6 Advanced fingering – note muting

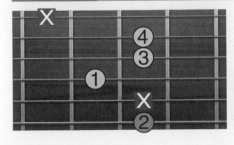

Moveable Chords

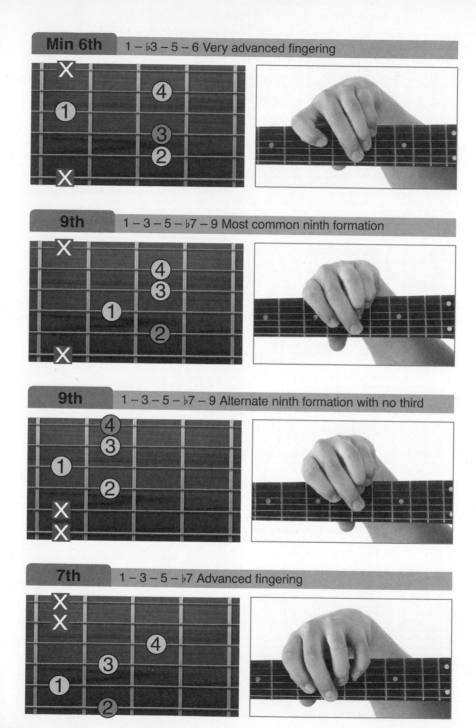

Min 6th 1 – ♭3 – 5 – 6 Very advanced fingering

9th 1 – 3 – 5 – ♭7 – 9 Most common ninth formation

9th 1 – 3 – 5 – ♭7 – 9 Alternate ninth formation with no third

7th 1 – 3 – 5 – ♭7 Advanced fingering

Moveable Chords

7aug9
1 – 3 – 5 – ♭7 – #9 Known as the 'Jimi Chord' after Jimi Hendrix

6/9
1 – 3 – 5 – 6 – 9 Very advanced fingering

Min 9th
1 – ♭3 – 5 – ♭7 – 9 Very advanced fingering

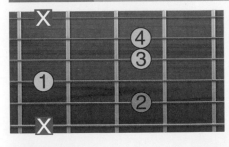

13th
1 – 3 – 5 – ♭7 – 9 – 13 Very advanced fingering

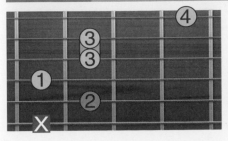

Moveable Chords

Major   1 – 3 – 5 Barred version of the open E major formation

7th   1 – 3 – 5 – ♭7 Barred version of the open E7 formation

7th   1 – 3 – 5 – ♭7 Barred version of alternate E7 formation

Minor   1 – ♭3 – 5 Barred version of the open E minor formation

Moveable Chords

212

Min 7th | 1 – ♭3 – 5 – ♭7 Derived from open E minor 7 formation

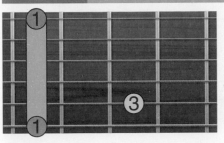
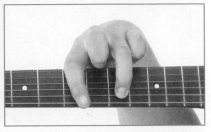

Min 7th | 1 – ♭3 – 5 – ♭7 Derived from alternate E minor 7 formation

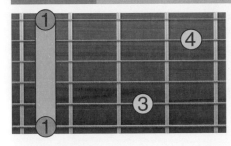

6th | 1 – 3 – 5 – 6 Derived from open E6 formation

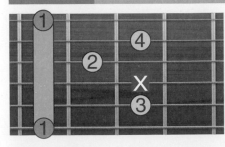

sus4 | 1 – 4 – 5 Derived from open Esus4 formation

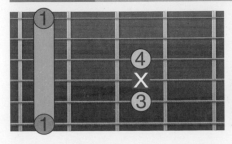
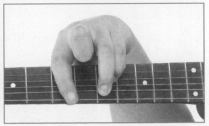

Moveable Chords

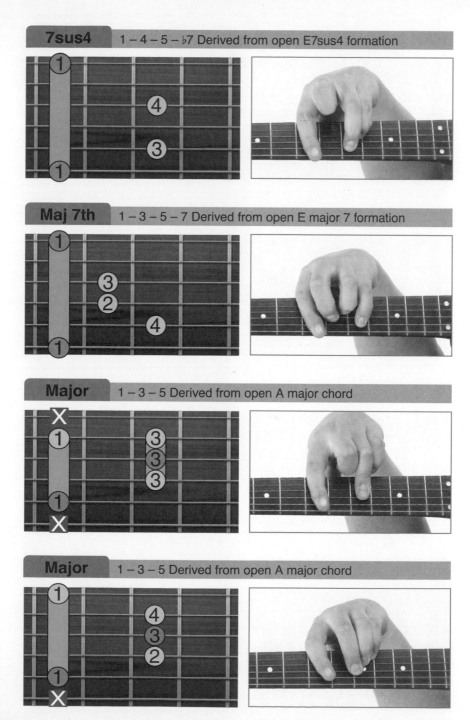

7sus4 1 – 4 – 5 – ♭7 Derived from open E7sus4 formation

Maj 7th 1 – 3 – 5 – 7 Derived from open E major 7 formation

Major 1 – 3 – 5 Derived from open A major chord

Major 1 – 3 – 5 Derived from open A major chord

1 – 3 – 5 – b7 Derived from open A7 chord

7th 1 – 3 – 5 – b7 Derived from alternate open A7 chord

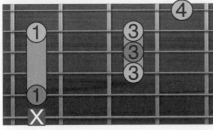

2/24/10 3:26:23 PM

Minor 1 – b3 – 5 Derived from open A minor chord

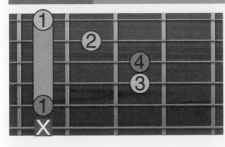

Min 7th 1 – b3 – 5 – b7 Derived from open A minor 7 chord

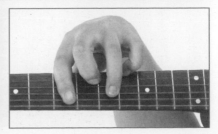

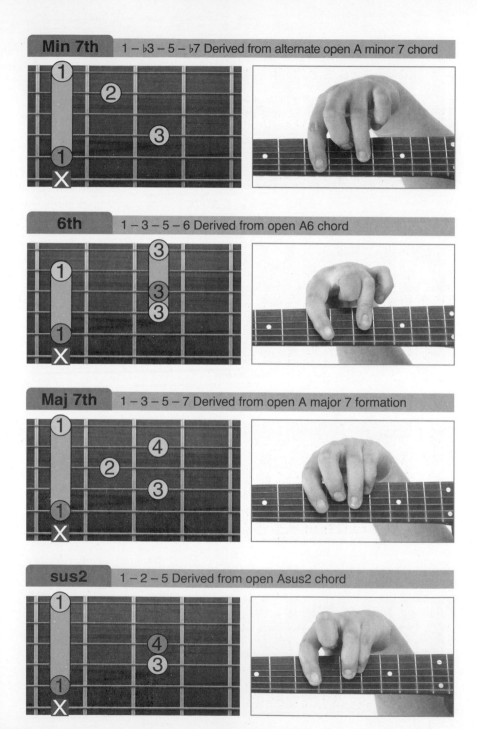

Min 7th
1 – ♭3 – 5 – ♭7 Derived from alternate open A minor 7 chord

6th
1 – 3 – 5 – 6 Derived from open A6 chord

Maj 7th
1 – 3 – 5 – 7 Derived from open A major 7 formation

sus2
1 – 2 – 5 Derived from open Asus2 chord

Major 1 – 3 – 5 Derived from open A major

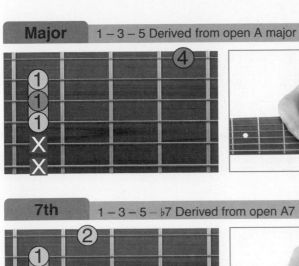

7th 1 – 3 – 5 – ♭7 Derived from open A7

Minor 1 – ♭3 – 5 Derived from open D minor chord

Major 1 – 3 – 5 – 7 Derived from open A

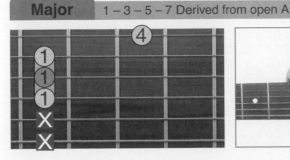

217

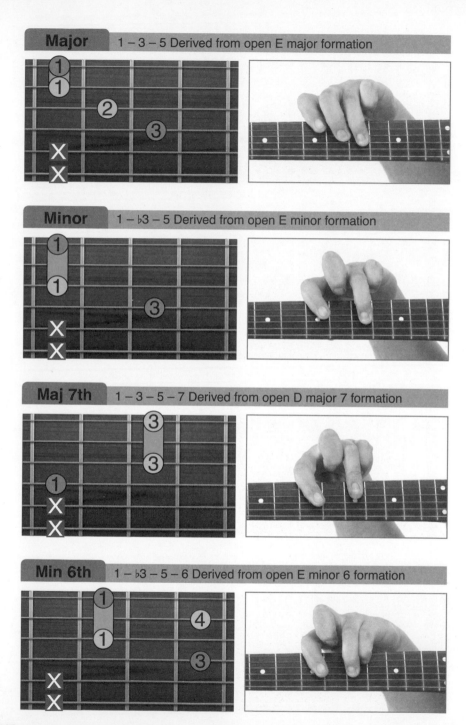

Major — 1 – 3 – 5 Derived from open E major formation

Minor — 1 – ♭3 – 5 Derived from open E minor formation

Maj 7th — 1 – 3 – 5 – 7 Derived from open D major 7 formation

Min 6th — 1 – ♭3 – 5 – 6 Derived from open E minor 6 formation

Major | 1 – 3 – 5 Derived from open A major formation

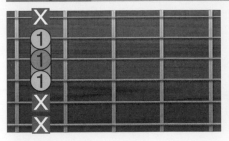

Minor | 1 – ♭3 – 5 Derived from open E minor: funk and reggae

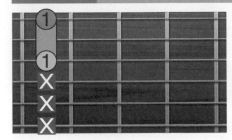
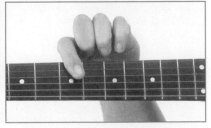

Major | 1 – 3 – 5 Derived from open C major formation

Maj 7th | 1 – 3 – 5 – 7 Derived from open C major 7 formation

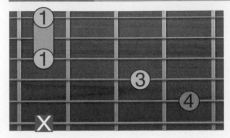
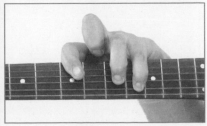

Moveable Chords

Power Chord 1 – 5 Based on open E: two notes barred

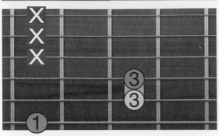 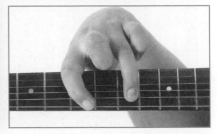

Power Chord 1 – 5 Based on open E: each note fingered

Power Chord 1 – 5 Based on open E: two note power chord

Power Chord 1 – 5 Based on open A: two notes barred

 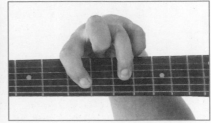

Moveable Chords

220

Power Chord 1 – 5 Based on open A: each note fingered

Power Chord 1 – 5 Based on open A: two note power chord

Power Chord 1 – 5 Based on open D: two note power chord

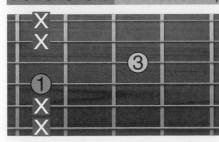

Power Chord 1 – 5 Based on open D: each note fingered

221

Moveable Chords

Guitar Scales

A Major Scale

A	B	C#	D	E	F#	G#	A
I	II	III	IV	V	VI	VII	I
1st	2nd	3rd	4th	5th	6th	7th	8th
	9th		11th		13th		

B♭ Major Scale

B♭	C	D	E♭	F	G	A	B♭
I	II	III	IV	V	VI	VII	I
1st	2nd	3rd	4th	5th	6th	7th	8th
	9th		11th		13th		

B Major Scale

B	C#	D#	E	F#	G#	A#	B
I	II	III	IV	V	VI	VII	I
1st	2nd	3rd	4th	5th	6th	7th	8th
	9th		11th		13th		

C Major Scale

C	D	E	F	G	A	B	C
I	II	III	IV	V	VI	VII	I
1st	2nd	3rd	4th	5th	6th	7th	8th
	9th		11th		13th		

C# Major Scale

C#	D#	E# (F)	F#	G#	A#	B# (C)	C#
I	II	III	IV	V	VI	VII	I
1st	2nd	3rd	4th	5th	6th	7th	8th
	9th		11th		13th		

D Major Scale

D	E	F#	G	A	B	C#	D
I	II	III	IV	V	VI	VII	I
1st	2nd	3rd	4th	5th	6th	7th	8th
	9th		11th		13th		

E♭ Major Scale

E♭	F	G	A♭	B♭	C	D	E♭
I	II	III	IV	V	VI	VII	I
1st	2nd	3rd	4th	5th	6th	7th	8th
	9th		11th		13th		

E Major Scale

E	F#	G#	A	B	C#	D#	E
I	II	III	IV	V	VI	VII	I
1st	2nd	3rd	4th	5th	6th	7th	8th
	9th		11th		13th		

F Major Scale

F	G	A	B♭	C	D	E	F
I	II	III	IV	V	VI	VII	I
1st	2nd	3rd	4th	5th	6th	7th	8th
	9th		11th		13th		

F# Major Scale

F#	G#	A#	B	C#	D#	E# (F)	F#
I	II	III	IV	V	VI	VII	I
1st	2nd	3rd	4th	5th	6th	7th	8th
	9th		11th		13th		

A♭ Major Scale

A♭	B♭	C	D♭	E♭	F	G	A♭
I	II	III	IV	V	VI	VII	I
1st	2nd	3rd	4th	5th	6th	7th	8th
	9th		11th		13th		

G Major Scale

G	A	B	C	D	E	F#	G
I	II	III	IV	V	VI	VII	I
1st	2nd	3rd	4th	5th	6th	7th	8th
	9th		11th		13th